DESIGNING WITH GLASS

GREAT GLASS BUILDINGS

50 MODERN CLASSICS

DESIGNING WITH GLASS

GREAT GLASS

BUILDINGS

50 MODERN
CLASSICS

PETER HYATT

ACKNOWLEDGEMENTS

Building is so often about mass, muscle and money. The architecture in this book offers an altogether different perspective. Crystaline forms of diamond clarity have an irresistible appeal. Their value is in the quality of the idea rather than the small idea inflated to bursting point. *Great Glass Buildings* features work that invites a rare curiosity and wonder. We are grateful to the featured architects whose work conveys such an uplifting, welcoming expression in an age of growing insecurity.

Such inventive problem solving requires equally brave and adventurous clients prepared to contribute to the design process; helping the architect to extract more than seemed possible. These clients have also generously opened their properties for this project.

Bankrolling design extends to the business of books. In a world fraught with risky business, publishing anything other than designer recipes, diets and wealth creation schemes is probably a form of commercial insanity. The Images Publishing Group is the world's fourth largest publisher of architecture; a fact not widely known or appreciated locally, but better understood internationally. IMAGES has championed the role and output of design for more than two decades and this book is a small part of a most formidable construction.

Book editors frequently save as many reputations as they make and Eliza Hope provided an invaluable role in this regard by ensuring the essential cohesion and consistency. Numerous photographers contributed to this book and we are also grateful for their generous spirit and compelling art.

This is a travelling exhibition and record of architecture as contemporary artefact. It represents many of the more inclusive, generous aspects of architecture as window instead of wall; bridge instead of barrier.

Peter and Jennifer Hyatt, 2004

First published in Australia in 2004 by The Images Publishing Group Pty Ltd
ABN 89 059 734 431
6 Bastow Place, Mulgrave, Victoria, 3170, Australia
Telephone: + 61 3 9561 5544 Facsimile: + 61 3 9561 4860
Email: books@images.com.au
Website: www.imagespublishinggroup.com
Copyright © The Images Publishing Group Pty Ltd
The Images Publishing Group Reference Number: 386

National Library of Australia
Cataloguing-in-Publication data

Hyatt, Peter.
Great glass buildings.

Includes index.
ISBN 1 86470 112 9.

1. Glass construction. 2. Architecture, Modern – 20th century. I. Hyatt, Jennifer. II. Title.

721.04496

Coordinating Editor: Eliza Hope

Designed by The Graphic Image Studio Pty Ltd, Mulgrave, Australia
Website: www.tgis.com.au

Film by Mission Productions Limited
Printed by Everbest Printing Co. Ltd, in Hong Kong/China

IMAGES has included on its website a page for special notices in relation to this and our other publications. Please visit this site: www.imagespublishinggroup.com

CONTENTS

INTRODUCTION

Architecture of delicate grandeur is precious. It is the diamond in an often bleak urban experience. Design of real difference can enrich lives in unexpected ways. If we breathe more easily in such places it is because magical spaces possess qualities that heighten our sense of wellbeing. Exceptional architecture rarely surfaces in a metropolis. Or anywhere. Great design is the exception to the rule. Architecture is widely discussed, but the real thing is all too rarely produced. No less exceptional is structure of rare touch and real empathy. A clutch of absorbing exceptions has emerged during the past few years and it suggests architecture is alive and well. The past decade has revealed a new attitude that is less monumental and faceless. The spirit of modernism prevails, but the mood is less prescriptive and tied to formula. Space, form, function and materials are being explored at an accelerating rate. Architecture has a renewed spirit and almost anything is possible.

Glass has become crucial to this architecture of optimism and levitation. If marble and stone symbolise Renaissance architecture, glass is the DNA of the new modernity. In the hands of special talent, glass transcends utility and the mere act of building. It would be simplistic to view the new modernism as merely a preoccupation with transparency. These lightweight forms and energy-efficient solutions can be highly expressive, technically challenging and audacious. No matter how clever the architecture, it must address the relationship between people, form and spaces. Do they connect?

Glass is giftwrap and lightweight armour in one. It provides transparency, ambiguity or opacity, layered with the possibility of intrigue and nuance. This mediation between spaces and environmental zones sees glass as transmitter and insulator. Not all projects in *Great Glass Buildings* enjoy an Arcadian setting, yet there is an art in finding opportunity in adversity. In the case of a sublime location they fully grasp the possibilities. Many buyers of architecture demand ponderous structures, making weight and size a priority. There is a certain irreverence about building lightly that is lost on those clients and architects who confuse quantity with quality. Modest in size but ambitious in scope, many of these projects are proof that the big idea made small is far preferable to the small idea blown out of all proportion. Whether exuberant, tranquil, elegantly poised or heightened by juxtaposition, glass is an essential component in space made magical by light.

As our natural environment shrinks and disappears, it is natural that many people should cling to that which remains. There is a responsibility that should partner development, and architecture needs to be an active participant in the process. The urban sprawl does not need to be ugly and difficult to negotiate; it can provide a beacon between the natural and

'Art lives by its skeleton ... grasp the skeleton and you can grasp the art.'
– Le Corbusier

synthetic. The soaring office tower can be an inspirational or drab neighbour. Small space can also be thrilling in its generosity and imagination. Do we have an attitude that is open or closed?

The featured projects are hallmarked by a technical and poetic resonance. These are not merely objects to be given the cursory inspection, but are frequently gorgeous to appraise. With this work there is plenty to intrigue. Where materials provide the physical skeleton, a masterly use of glass creates architecture with gleaming eyes and luminous soul. In this regard the new modernism considers space in the three dimensions, thereby releasing glass from its stereotypical, planar role as window dressing. Transmission, reflection and refraction generate challenges as well as opportunities, thus the harnessing of daylight remains one of architecture's greatest challenges. Corbusier's vivacious form and space-making at Ronchamp (1954) and Dominican Friary at La Tourette (1960) demonstrate the magician's touch. Even in small measure, Corbusier could telescope enormous energy through glass: 'The key is light and light illuminates shapes and shapes have an emotional power'. To design well it is necessary to conceptualise and draw with delicate force. This paradox, that the effort may be great but the touch of necessity light, is easily overlooked.

Two factors have dramatically influenced glass usage since modernism's apogee in the mid 20th century. Advances in glass-making technology and computers now permit far more complex technical solutions. Such luxuries were simply unavailable when Mies van der Rohe conceived the glass curtain wall for his prescient and elegantly curvaceous *Friedrichstrasse* tower for Berlin in 1921. This was one of many instances where building technology was unable to match the early modernist vision. None of this daunted the dream of evaporating walls of frameless glass that dissolved into the clouds. By 1929 Mies was already on the ground floor with the exploded space and dissolved boundaries of his skeletal Barcelona Pavilion at the International Exposition.

During the 1990s glass began its re-emergence. It had been relegated to the wilderness during the efflorescence of postmodernism. For many, the anonymous glass curtain wall helped accelerate modernism's demise, but echoes of original ideas are hard to snuff out. Something endured and practices such as **Foster Associates**, **Future Systems** and **Kengo Kuma** persevered with their own brands of humane modernism. They symbolised an intuitive mastery of light and space. This momentum has gathered with the new millennium. The small resonant form is suddenly as important as the towering statement. If nothing else, the new modernism is concerned with habitable, humane spaces. Unlike early modernism, the new incarnation is much less about doctrine and imposed form. These are exemplars that make the leap from the dreary monolith to sculptured geometry.

Some forms are exuberant, others introspective. Lightly sheathed yet deceptively strong, they shape as potent signatures of the era. The gossamer elegance of glass is seductive. When so much around appears leaden and earth-bound, occupants of the great glass building are illuminated and transported. Ordinary communities are suddenly benefiting from the creation of energised, luminous buildings. The upfront cost of the prototype may appear negative in the eyes of accountants, but the bankrolling of inventive architecture can pay huge cultural and social dividends. Increasingly clients are looking for function and pleasurable space rather than the mass and status of the fortress.

It is hardly coincidental that glass is a constant in much of the new modernism. Natural light transmission and visual connectedness can contribute gains in workplace safety, productivity and sense of wellbeing. Many of those projects with articulated and expressed glass skins arouse a disproportionately strong level of curiosity that is only now beginning to be better understood. Architecture that confronts and contradicts mainstream work needs to withstand levels of scrutiny rarely applied to nondescript and poor design. Elegance and power often attract attention for the wrong reason. Tawdry buildings are regularly overlooked, forgotten or forgiven more readily than work of dynamic difference. The community can easily be divided by a new neighbour. Real design requires inspired drivers and resolute clients. Architecture is nothing if not difficult in the pursuit of innovative, fresh perspectives.

The emerging aesthetic of the glass skin has a strong humanist element that continues the legacy provided by work of the early and mid 20th century. The influence of the modern masters echoes throughout *Great Glass Buildings* even if once lofty, utopian ideals now appear naive and, in many ways, inappropriate. The new modernism is infinitely more complex in conception and a response to humanistic, thermal and environmental issues. Multiple glass façades, metallic glass coating, seraphic finishes and a lightweight armoury of baffles, screens, louvres and scrims are utilised for sun shading, sustainable design and expressed identity. Many building designers treat daylight as an enemy thus relegating occupants to a twilight world of flickering neon tubing. At the other extreme vast, unshaded expanses of glass can create almost incurable glare and thermal management issues. Recent examples retain the drive for a pristine aesthetic, but better bridge concept and reality through advances in glass-making and construction technology. Early 20th-century visions of glass towers were impossible to realise because of technological limitations. The advent of structural glazing, fixing systems, glass coatings and waterproof connections allow for symmetry between ambition and achievement. The building skin is increasingly critical as we strive for more responsible built environments that maximise energy efficiency. Workplaces can be much more productive, comfortable and safer when users are better able to manage their immediate working environment. Other benefits also occur. Lower carbon dioxide emissions are being achieved in buildings that cut their reliance on energy-guzzling appliances. New glazing techniques and types are making possible many of the new forms, but building materials can only achieve so much. Ultimately energy performance and comfort levels require total design integrity rather than the corrective, applied solution.

Today's master architect would never attempt to divine a design without exhaustive research into client and occupant aspirations. Great design may be simple, but it is never simplistic. True simplicity requires enormous effort. Many of the featured projects illustrate that submission and integration of site are more important than domination. Architecture, in many ways, is an irreducible art. The magical in one place does not necessarily transplant for a whole range of reasons that include culture, environment and climate.

Sustainable design is now an inescapable reality as much as it looms as the cliché. Will design to regulation standards ever produce the epiphany? Incidentals such as tapware, bench tops and joinery, while important, are not the central issues vying for their designers' attention. Smart appliances, furnishings and high-tech gadgets might complement great design, but can they also disguise architecture's lesser achievements? This is one reason that many architects prefer to lead their clients towards philosophical design issues. Many featured projects have ambitious form such that their builders and engineers must have had sleepless nights. Such is the contribution of many teams of contractors and materials suppliers to achieve the final vision.

The new modernism explores the oblique and discreet transparency. Flexible outer, inter and inner layers offer the benefits of subtlety as well as exposure. In addition to free spans, glass-clad structures now benefit from technologies that support the trend to sustainable design. New glazing systems and coatings are incorporated in the design attitude towards environmental and climatic response. In this regard glass developments include self-cleaning, photovoltaic, adjustable transparency, low solar emission and multi-coated varieties. In combination with dual skins, structures that would normally require extensive mechanical heating or cooling provide all of the benefits of natural light with few of the usual penalties. The principles of fresh air being ducted into work or living spaces are essentially the same, whereby cool or warm air as required is drawn through openings in the structural walls and into the negatively pressured façade plenum.

Other measures including louvres, mixed-mode ventilation systems utilising natural ventilation and integrated thermal flues are being used to accelerate air movement. Interior planning principles must also be tied into the strategy for maximum cross-ventilation perimeter circulation and open-plan work areas. Walls of filtered natural light cut the dependence on artificial lighting, cooling and heating for all but the most extreme conditions. Resistant to high summer sun, embracing of lower winter light and beautifully ventilated, the projects embody the concept of fit, healthy workspaces.

Many commercial projects allow employees to select airflow with pinpoint accuracy through floor and window slots. Such flexibility offers a multitude of energy-saving and comfort benefits over standard air-conditioning practice. Major urban power failures highlight the failure level of dependence on energy-guzzling devices and the need to explore alternative energy sources in the face of greenhouse gas emissions and dependence on fossil fuels. Despite anxieties about global terrorism, there is usually no need for higher, stronger and bigger walls. In all but extreme cases, transparency opens the way to engagement. This can say a great deal about an organisation. Modern management is only just coming to grips with the benefits of employees empowered by choice. Instead of a soporific, one-size-fits-all workplace, an imaginative strategy generates improved comfort, safety and productivity levels.

There is an optimism when bold ideas are married with new technologies. The projects in *Great Glass Buildings* speak of today, but shape as talismans for tomorrow. It is architecture that refers to the past, but points towards the future. The work appears futuristic because, like its modernist precursor, it rejects the conventions of spatial clutter and hierarchy. Yet old-fashioned values of craft and tradition inevitably prevail. Direct expression and appropriate technology count for much. This new modernism varies from being overt in its expression to flirtatious when the subject is hardly more than a floating veil.

The distilled clarity of glass can startle as well as tantalise. Many of the projects on wider public view generate debate and attract notice. They are challenging and different. Criticism of

glass as skin often results from misunderstanding or ignorance. Issues such as thermal and noise management as well as privacy have created doubts among those who see such creations as fish tank or peep show. Many of the projects are contentious because they challenge perceptions about privacy and personal space. At its best the new modernism achieves a fully three-dimensional quality that is difficult to replicate and franchise. The selected projects are an acute response to place. They are purpose-built and achieve a rare serendipity.

Architecture can never exist in a vacuum and this is especially true of its relationship with big business. Pressure for increased levels of financial propriety is adding to the groundswell for greater levels of transparency, openness and disclosure. Corporate malpractice and collapses have done little for levels of public trust and confidence. The mood for positive revelation is also a response to doubts aroused by misadventures within the edifice. Privacy and confidentiality are a necessary part of business, so a balance must be struck to help create a culture of trust and confidence. Governments, institutions and organisations are increasingly obliged to reassess their public face as open or closed, friend or foe. The benefits of a more connected and accountable management and workforce should be obvious.

Perception of big business is changing in other areas. Banks and insurance companies no longer store huge reserves of hard currency. The transfer of funds is now essentially electronic and transactions occur more often via credit card and computer thereby freeing companies to adopt a more liberal, transparent position. Top-heavy management and overweight, overbearing institutions seem to have much in common. Hopefully example, and better education, will ensure more appropriately tuned forms prevail.

The invitation to read architecture as more than mass and motifs represents a powerful opportunity. *Great Glass Buildings* reflects an evolutionary leap of faith. Many of the architects and clients are fearless, not because they risk untested theories, but because they challenge zealous planning authorities vigilant to maintain anachronistic and flawed building codes.

X-ray architecture is hardly a risk-free strategy with failures and faults easily magnified and revealed. This partly explains the *faux* modesty and preference to cover up and dress the jigsaw of construction. Nevertheless glass provides a palpable substance lost on those who see building through the eyes of a merchant as a transferable commodity. There can be poetics of assembly where elegance is revealed by windows treated as much more than the hole left over by the builder. This is the language of the new modernism, notable for allowing a view into, or through, the object of desire rather than simply looking *at* an object. Modernism cracked the code and created an entirely different perspective and dimension. The turn of the new millennium seems to have triggered a rediscovery of the poetry in technology. So much so that glass-based structures are rapidly emerging as a unique genre. Big or small, public or private, the desire to link with other spaces and fabric, natural and synthetic is increasing.

Sir Joseph Paxton's Crystal Palace should be a dignified memory, but once the genie was released, return to the lamp was impossible. This hasn't been altogether a good thing. Imitators of such prodigious talent have clung shamelessly to his coat-tails ever since, and grubbied a fine garment in the process. Paxton's epoch-making was not a bad effort for gardener turned architect. The soil taught him more than an understanding of parsnips and petunias. He was the pioneer of prefabrication that ushered a new vocabulary of material and connections. In 1853, the year of the Crystal Palace's completion, the writer John Ruskin observed:

'No person who is not a great sculptor or painter can be an architect. If he is not a sculptor or painter, he can only be a builder.'

All great design is seized upon, but 120 years passed before commerce saw opportunity in his soaring glazed vaults. Paxton suddenly provided a light shaft in the gloom of city-making. The crystalline envelope was franchised as big top for a cocoon of velvetine upholstery, floral sprays and piped music. So began payday for hotel chains, casinos and shopping malls. Prophet one day, profit the next. It shouldn't require architecture of any quality to make the jump of more than a century, but it does in this instance, because Paxton was destined to be a time-traveller.

Groundbreakers such as Paxton, Mies, Le Corbusier, Richard Neutra and Charles and Ray Eames were among those prepared to challenge standard practise. There is a great joy in generous space-making and considered detailing that speaks of a love for their calling.

These were among the masters of material subtraction. They saw condensed energy when others could only see only clutter. This set new benchmarks for spatial continuity and redefined the elevated floor slab, prefabrication, floating stairs, slender mullions and frameless glass. They all understood the skeleton of art.

Each and every masterpiece spawns counterfeits thus the apothegm Less is More did not take long to sour into the handy convenience store of More or Less. Subtraction quickly becomes poverty in the wrong hands. Copyists adapted and borrowed with a fervour impressive for its opportunism. Towards the end of the 20th century, modernism had run its course. Something was missing in the mechanical response and imitation of the masters' voices. Mies' planar cubism, Corbusier's elemental constructivism and Wright's organic energies were being squandered in deals over which the originators had no control. Ultimately this paved the way for the speculative impact of postmodernism. Relief in this burlesque and often high-camp pastiche provided an unsatisfying antidote for moribund business precincts. Architecture of the future will reflect many modernist preoccupations of structure stripped of arbitrary language that functions as the sustainable object. Architecture has an obligation to resist the temptation to constantly replicate its own creations and trade on successful patterns at the expense of creative risk taking. Prototypes can be time-consuming and expensive. Good reason then to respect rather than imitate the original ambition.

Great Glass Buildings is a distillation of outstanding contemporary architecture from around the world. It is evidence of a positive information transfer. There is an often overlooked aspect of globalisation that involves the shared idea. Evidence perhaps that the trend is not wholly bad or negative. Good ideas travel fast too. Glass offers refuge and prospect. Its environmental flexibility connects most directly to the invisible qualities of place such as breezes, scents and sounds. This selective connection to place can heighten the positive experiences and modify the unappealing. If we have learned

anything from modern architecture, it is the importance of humane, habitable space. Wholesale transparency isn't for everyone. Hermits and Howard Hughes types need not apply. Selective transparency considered as part of a bigger whole can transform space, light and life. There is one argument for the clever diagram, elegant drawing and sharp aesthetics, but safe, comfortable conditions are something else altogether.

Architecture is at its most potent when people become self aware. Good design fundamentally exists on an emotional plane and good design brings those emotions to the surface. Architecture that promotes an emotional and spiritual awareness is inevitably good architecture, irrespective of style. Shining examples are not necessarily the heroic, blockbuster variety. Some are found tucked away in unlikely parts of city and country. Often highly unlikely, they juxtapose and respect the existing built fabric or connect mellifluously to their place. They convey an optimism and exuberance. They may even inspire. Not all are expensive prototypes. Many use simple, off-the-rack materials and prove that not every detail needs to be customised with capricious spending to achieve a high plane of architecture.

The great modernists could only hold centre stage for so long, but they proved that architecture could be made to appear effortless and an entirely appropriate response. Architecture has a metaphor in ballet. The great modernists were equivalent to the sensual power and technique of ballet's superstars Nijinsky, Barishnikov and Nureyev. Whether coiled to spring, or floating, here was architecture of the sky rather than the earth. No longer rooted in the past, architecture had a new point of reference. Filigree structure and glass created the dissolving assembly of light, lighter, lightest. This was architecture that danced. There was no looking back.

The new modernism is no less aspirational. Great Glass Buildings reveals delight in the illuminated, magical form and space. Whether private or public, these projects trigger a strong human response to the temporal, spiritual and physical worlds. Work as diverse as teahouse, private residence, public spa and grand civic gesture indicates new modernism's appeal. There are countless obstacles to the achievement of great architecture and this, quite simply, explains its short supply.

Architecture schools around the world produce a seemingly endless supply line of new practitioners. In the end it is an alchemy of vision, client, site, persistence and relevance that allows dreams to materialise. There is something utterly irresistible and cathartic about the dream transformed. Art, engineering, science and the human experience become one in Great Glass Buildings – all the more reason to celebrate those who light the way. None of these architects should fear or fret about falling behind. They are already light years ahead.

Peter Hyatt and Jennifer Hyatt
Editors

MODERN CLASSICS

1

2

3

30 St Mary Axe

4

1 Panoramic view of the city from across the River Thames
2 General view of the building
3 Elevation
4 View from Lime Street
5 Site plan

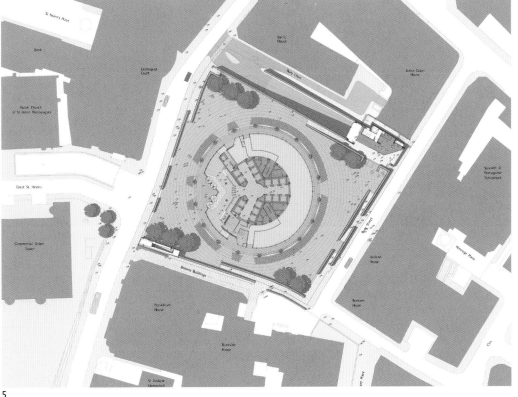

5

LONDON, UNITED KINGDOM | ARCHITECT: FOSTER AND PARTNERS
STRUCTURAL ENGINEER: ARUP | 2004

30 St Mary Axe is located on the former site of the Baltic Exchange in the City of London. The distinctive form of the 40-storey office tower adds to the cluster of tall buildings that symbolises the heart of London's financial centre. It is the capital's first environmentally progressive tall building. 30 St Mary Axe is not only an office building; its street level is publicly accessible with double-height retail outlets that serve the local working community, and the building is set within a new public plaza.

At the top of the building are private dining and corporate hospitality facilities for the building's occupants and their guests. Beneath the glazed dome a restaurant offers spectacular westerly views. The restaurant's mezzanine – a flexible space for drinks, gatherings and presentations – has a full 360-degree view panorama over the city and beyond. The building is radical – technically, architecturally, socially and spatially. Both from the outside and from within it is unlike any office building so far conceived.

The building has a circular plan that widens as it rises from the ground and then tapers towards its apex. This form responds to the specific demands of the small site. The building appears less bulky than a conventional rectangular block of equivalent floor area; the slimming of the building's profile at its base reduces reflections, improves transparency and increases daylight penetration at ground level. Mid-height, the floor-plates offer larger areas of office accommodation; the tapering apex of the tower minimises the extent of reflected sky.

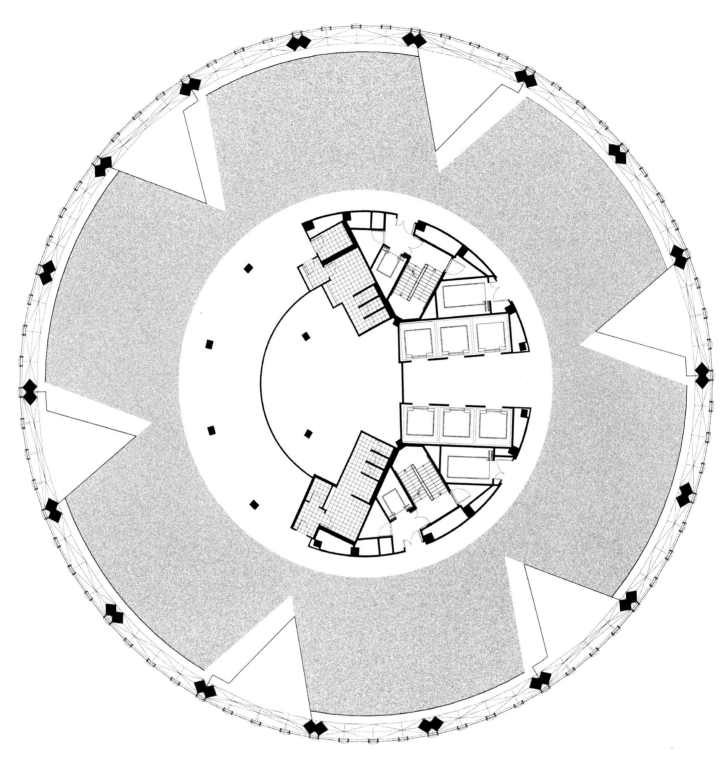

6

The aerodynamic form encourages wind to flow around its face, minimising wind loads on the structure and cladding, enabling the use of a more efficient structure. Wind is not deflected to ground level – as it is with rectilinear buildings – helping to maintain pedestrian comfort and safety at the base of the building. Wind tunnel tests have shown that the building will improve wind conditions in the vicinity. Natural air movement around the building generates substantial pressure differences across its face, which can be used to facilitate natural ventilation within the building.

The fully glazed skin of the building allows the occupants to enjoy increased external awareness and the benefits of daylight. The glazing of the office areas comprises two layers of glass with a cavity, which is ventilated by the used air drawn from the offices. This enables solar radiation to be intercepted before it reaches the office spaces to reduce the typically large air-conditioning load. The cladding of the lightwells consists of simple operable and fixed double-glazed panels with tinted glass and a high-performance coating to reduce the penetration of solar radiation.

8

6   Typical office floor plan
7   Section
8   Façade detail
Photography: Nigel Young/Foster and Partners

ATAMI WATER/GLASS RESIDENCE

1 Staircase well
2 View from glass bridge to Lounge
3 Sea side exterior view

ATAMI, SHIZUOKA PREFECTURE, JAPAN | ARCHITECT: KENGO KUMA
STRUCTURAL ENGINEER: K.NAKATA & ASSOCIATES | 1995

The design of this villa was greatly influenced by the Hyuga Villa, the sole project that Bruno Taut designed in Japan. The design was also influenced by the philosophy of Taut. Taut's stay in Japan lasted from 1933 until 1936, although his praise of Katsura Palace continues. The reasoning for this commendation can be found in the fact that the Palace frames nature, yet frames by being one with nature.

Taut paid specific attention to mechanisms in Katsura Palace that provoked the framing of nature with nature: the eaves and the bamboo verandas. Thus, in the Atami Villa, a layer of water that gently covers the building edges signifies the bamboo verandas in Katsura. Moreover, a stainless steel louvre that covers the water signifies the eaves. The water surface

stretches further out and unites the surface with the Pacific Ocean. And on top of the joined surface, a glass box floats. As the box is superimposed numerous times, refraction of materials brings in reflections of sorts. The relationship between the subject and the environment is challenged in various ways by redefining and reshaping the Katsura philosophy, yet always maintaining its fundamental essence.

I used steel-frame construction instead of concrete, even though the building incorporates a great deal of water, which makes detailing particularly difficult. My aim was to create a collection of particles composed of a steel-frame structure and stainless louvres – drifting on the surface of the water. The water surface also served as a device for generating sparkling

ATAMI WATER/GLASS RESIDENCE

4

particles of light. That was the first time I used such louvres. Since then, I have created louvres of various materials and various cross-sections. In Stone Museum (2000), I even tried to transform stone, a massive material, into a cloudlike substance by transforming it into particles.

In the Atami Villa I tried for the first time to create, not only a particulate condition through the use of louvres, but also a frame using horizontal planes. This building stands on a cliff; there is no point from which one can get an exterior view of the building. I decided therefore to disregard distant or bird's-eye-view of the building and to take into consideration only interior and ground-level views.

Furthermore, I tried planning the building using, not walls, but a horizontal plane (that is, the floor). In the Western architectural tradition, a building is primarily framed by means of walls and windows. That interposes a frame between the

subject and the object. The subject is inevitably cut off from the object. The space becomes a painting in a frame (that is, a static image); it becomes frozen. On the other hand, in traditional Japanese architecture, horizontal planes (that is, the floor and the ceiling) are the dominant framing devices. This enables the subject and the object to coexist in a continuous space, without being cut off from each other by the frame. In such a case, the main concern of planning is the introduction of a sequence and speed into continuous space. One cannot help but introduce into the building the parameter of time as well as the parameter of space. As a result, space takes on the character of a dynamic image, and space and time become inextricably entwined. In the Atami Villa, I tried to frame space with only two horizontal planes – the floor of water and the ceiling louvres – and to generate between the planes a transparent and fluid time-space.

4   Looking at lounge

5   View from lounge

6   Guestroom

7   1F Water court to Japanese room

5

6

7

ATAMI WATER/GLASS RESIDENCE

8

9

10

1

THE ATRIUM AT FEDERATION SQUARE

2

3

1 Entrance to north atrium from Flinders Street, looking south

2 North atrium cantilever, from Flinders Street looking east to NGV

3 BMW Edge (south atrium), looking to south to Yarra River, showing folded inner glazing skin Barrisol roof tiling and lighting system

MELBOURNE, VICTORIA, AUSTRALIA | ARCHITECT: LAB ARCHITECTURE STUDIO IN ASSOCIATION WITH BATES SMART
FAÇADE AND SPECIAL STRUCTURES ENGINEER: ATELIER ONE | 2002

Federation Square is Melbourne's new civic heart. A 3.6-hectare precinct of cultural and synergetic commercial activities, this award-winning project is constructed over railway lines, and is focused on two civic spaces. These are the new, undulating civic square, Melbourne's new public gathering and event space, and the continuously open, publicly accessible glazed and covered atrium.

The atrium is a unique covered public space, providing a complement to the open plaza. It is formed into two distinct elements, designated north atrium and south atrium (or 'BMW Edge'). As a continuously open, publicly accessible space, the atrium is emblematic of Federation Square's intended linkage of city and river, and reveals the 'permeable' nature of the project.

The north atrium, as a glazed covered street, provides a forecourt to the National Gallery of Victoria – Australia (NGV), with an open interior volume 16 metres high and up to 20 metres across. This glass-enclosed galleria is animated on the east side by the NGV's bookshop, cafe and restaurant facilities, and on the west side by additional retail and commercial outlets.

The north atrium is a civic gathering space for large, indoor events. In this mode, the space can be subdivided into a series of small, distinct stages for performance, including; live music, aerial trapeze artists, choral recitals and public speaking. The

4

5

6

atrium is the home for a regular cycle of events including markets, city festivals, exhibitions, civic dinners and corporate launches.

The BMW Edge (the south atrium) is a unique flexible performance venue, capable of working both independently and in concert with events in the north atrium. The BMW Edge has two modes: street mode and performance. In street mode, it is a glass-enclosed street animated by a cafe on the northern edge. Patrons can enjoy lunch, either seated on the steps of the Ironbark Amphitheatre or on a glass walkway threaded through the atrium structure, with views overlooking the Yarra River.

In performance mode, the BMW Edge hosts both ticketed and non-ticketed events. In ticketed performance mode, it is isolated from the noise and activity of the north atrium via a large, folding acoustic door. An audience of up to 467 is seated in Ironbark seats designed specifically for this atrium. The inner glass skin of the atrium is turned inward to form a glass topography that follows the complex, three-dimensional framework of the atrium structure. Together with a variety of finely perforated Barrisol tiles, the venue has been designed to provide an acoustic profile precisely tuned for high-quality music performances.

The open galvanised structural frames of the atrium evolved from the same triangular geometry as that of the façades, but developed as a folded three-dimensional system glazed both inside and out. The deep space of this supporting frame acts

as a thermal chimney, evacuating the build-up of hot air. The atrium space itself is conditioned by a passive cooling system, using a low level air-displacement system to keep the comfort zone of the atrium up to 12 degrees Celsius cooler than the outside temperature in summer. It is an environmentally sustainable system that uses one-tenth of the energy consumption compared to conventional cooling systems, while emitting only one-tenth of the carbon dioxide gases.

The glazing system is a suspended chain net – an irregular curtain wall of galvanised steel-framed pinwheel shapes, laterally restrained at more or less regular intervals from the primary structure. Each aluminium-framed glass tile is supported by a corresponding galvanised steel frame, each frame is then bolted to its neighbour, forming a light steel lattice work.

The atrium is glazed with an inner and an outer skin. The outer skin is a rain-screen made from a single glazed solar glass with a very light tint. The inner sealed skin is made from double glazed units incorporating a low-e film.

For all of the apparent irregularity of the glass framing, the glazed skins are tiled by only nine different shapes, based on various configurations of pinwheel triangle units. The triangular geometry allows for this variation and gives a high degree of visual interest, while still being constructed by a very ordered and repetitive system. 950 separate tiles glaze an area of over 4,300 square metres across the inner and outer glass skins.

4   North atrium, west wall, showing inner and outer glazing skins and primary structure

5   North atrium to cantilever, looking south to NGV entrance, showing restaurant and retail area on right

6   Looking up the north atrium to cantilever and Flinders Street entrance, showing primary structure and Barrisol roof tiling

7   BMW Edge (south atrium), east elevation, looking to Yarra River and Victorian Arts Centre

8   BMW Edge (south atrium), east elevation, showing outer glazing and primary structure, looking west to Yarra River and city

9   North atrium, west wall outer glazing detail, showing pinwheel tiling of glazing units and primary structure, reflection of façade of the Australian Centre for the Moving Image (left) and Melbourne skyline (right)

Photography: Peter Hyatt

7

8

9

1

AUSTRIAN SCHOOL
(ÖSTERREICHISCHE SCHULE)

1 Hall
2 Northwest elevation
3 East elevation

2

3

BUDAPEST, HUNGARY | ARCHITECT: GEORG DRIENDL ARCHITEKT
STRUCTURAL ENGINEER: D.I. MAC WALLNÖFER | 2001

The Austrian School in Budapest is an obviously contemporary, open, light-flooded glass appliance that slides up beside a banal school building dating from the 19th century. The project was planned as a three-wing building placed on an approximately north–south axis. The side wings are occupied by classrooms, teachers' offices and a stairway on the west side. The side wings are more bulky, whereas the middle section of the building, containing hallways, toilets and elevators for handicapped students, is narrower. The uncovered concrete surfaces are most dominant in the middle section, which is the solid core of the building. The structures get lighter towards the

front walls. The central core is a three-storey-high hall that is completely glazed. It is also where the roof-plates meet (they jut out above the wall surfaces, which makes them appear light).

The logic of the arrangement is that architectural structures get lighter towards the façades. Parallel to this, the floor space of the various sections gets bigger and bigger as one approaches the external world through the front walls. This is a highly symbolic architectural path connecting school and life. It is the result of a future-oriented approach, in contrast with the isolating tendency in traditional school buildings.

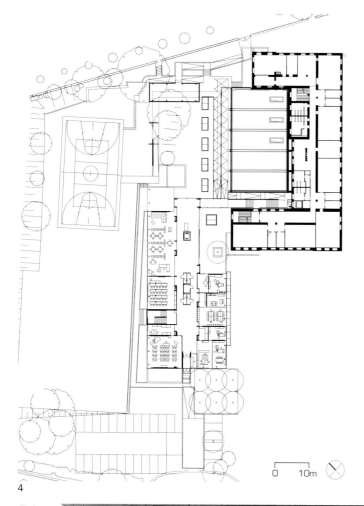

4   Ground floor plan
5   Hall – first floor
6   Sports facilities
7   Southwest elevation – entrance

Photography: Pez Hejduk; James Morris/Axiom photo agency

4

5

6

Partly due to this gesture, and partly for the purpose of loosening up the tube-like central section, the roof structures behind the steel-supported glass façade open into each other, creating an atrium. It is a smart solution that the elevator shaft has a glass wall in the direction of the façade with the atrium, following the opening-up-from-inside arrangement and showing the mechanism of the elevator in full.

The classrooms are large, with full-height windows letting in much light, shaded by sturdy aluminium lamellas in three rows on the sunny side, together with galvanised-lattice passage galleries, the first layer of an enthrallingly new constructivist frontal composition. The classroom partition walls do not run solid up to the curtain wall plane, but connect to it via a window section. Another window, at the top, makes the connection to the ceiling, and yet another, above the inward-reaching wide

reinforced concrete frieze, in the direction of the corridor. This gives a feeling of openness and transparency.

The building itself is a low energy house with several environmentally conscious features, unusual in Hungary, such as the recycling of rainwater. The balconies in front of the classrooms (this is probably the only school in the county where classrooms have balconies) are not only a very popular place for students to take their breaks, they also make the rooms seem wider and – due to the two balcony doors – provide a special ventilation system.

As a result of all this it is no surprise that most of the pupils of the senior high school feel extremely well in this building. According to the headmaster, the new building has increased the delight in learning to an unbelievable extent, a fact also confirmed in the school exams.

AUSTRIAN SCHOOL (ÖSTERREICHISCHE SCHULE)

1

BARK DESIGN STUDIO

2

3

4

1 The eastern glazed façade and automated external fabric blinds open to the views, whilst providing flexible open configurations for maximum comfort, with natural cooling breezes drawn through glass louvres into the workspace and extracted through the mezzanine / loft spaces above

2 The glazed steel-framed studio slots between two mature Australian eucalypts as it cantilevers above the sloping terrain

3 The operable glazed end floats alongside the trunk of one of the 'sacred' mature Australian eucalypts

4 The open linear 'veranda-type' workspace

NOOSA, QUEENSLAND, AUSTRALIA | ARCHITECT: BARK DESIGN
STRUCTURAL ENGINEER: TOD NOOSA | 2001

B ark Design partners Stephen Guthrie and Lindy Atkin's brief for themselves was to 'showcase' their design approach whilst making an inspiring place to work for the Bark Design team and their clients.

Elevated as a modernist steel and glass pavilion in the Noosa Hinterland, the Sunshine Coast-based duo have created a glass studio as the work environment for their emerging architectural practice. The design strategy ensured flexibility between a space for work and a space for living and various combinations of both – resulting in a 'workhouse' typology.

Perched on four steel footings in order to slot between two mature Australian eucalypts, the modular 20-metre-long structure of steel portal frames is encased with openable and fixed glazing on three sides, layered with operable blinds, framing the broad views of the Pacific coastline of Queensland's Northern Sunshine Coast. The fourth façade is presented as the 'billboard', a plywood-clad wooden box facing the road, providing privacy, protection from the western sun, a desired ambiguity of perceived use and a big 'drive-in movie' projection screen. The solid nature of this form is punctured with horizontal glass slots and is contrasted with the northern timber entry platforms and horizontal roof planes, which simply provide lightweight steel framing of the landscape beyond.

BARK DESIGN STUDIO

5

6

The main linear workspace was conceived as an open veranda with compactly scaled service spaces 'plugging in' along its length. From the main studio platform, folded plywood stairs ascend past the large 'shopfront' window box, displaying models of past and current projects to a mezzanine level, which contains spaces for architecture books, quiet reading, sleeping and bathing. From this mezzanine, there is a spatial, visual connection to ventilate the work spaces below whilst presenting a 'cropped' horizontal framing of the hinterland and coastal horizon beyond.

The desired concept of lightly visually 'floating' the building above the natural ground line (in part, to minimise any disturbance to the natural ground line) by using only four supports, became necessary in order to maintain the extended root systems of the two magnificent mature trees.

The modular design was developed using a series of 3.6- and 4.8-metre structural grids to incorporate the 1,200-millimetre standard size of 'infill' materials for plywood sheet walls, floors and ceilings. The steel and glass aesthetic creates a 'legible structural order' and a generously proportioned series of simple modest spaces.

At every junction, glass surfaces are simply juxtaposed with steel, aluminium, timber and plywood with clear, honest expression of materials and a clear legibility of structure.

7

8

5 Mezzanine space for reading, sleeping and bathing with its 'cropped' horizontal framing of the landscape

6 Operable glazed meeting space embraces views across the Noosa Hinterland and out to the Pacific Ocean

7 Folded plywood stairs within the 'service' zone ascend to the mezzanine / loft spaces above

8 Northern timber platforms 'float' above the landscape, cantilevered from the 'billboard' plywood-clad box which faces the road to the west

Photography: Peter Hyatt

1

BRENTWOOD SKYTRAIN STATION

1   Night view from the west
2   Interior platform looking west
3   View from pedestrian ramp
4   View from mezzanine bridge

BURNABY, BRITISH COLUMBIA, CANADA │ ARCHITECT: BUSBY + ASSOCIATES
ARCHITECTS
STRUCTURAL ENGINEER: FAST & EPP PARTNERS │ 2002

Busby + Associates Architects were selected to design two skytrain stations for the Millennium Line of the Rapid Transit Project in the Greater Vancouver area. Both stations are designed to maximise safety, security and comfort for transit users. Essential elements are open, clear spaces, the use of glass for visibility and the provision of generous canopies for rain and wind protection. The intention is to encourage use of the transit system, through accessibility and safety. Both stations incorporate a high-tech look, with user-friendly warmth.

The Brentwood Station has been designed to be a flagship location in the new ALRT line. Adjacent to Brentwood Shopping Mall, it is a major transfer point to an existing bus loop, and

serves as a catalyst for redevelopment of the future Brentwood Town Centre. Its prominent location over the Lougheed Highway also provides an opportunity to make it a landmark above the road.

The design of the main station structure incorporates a sleek and dynamic enclosure for the station platform. As part of the long-term redevelopment there will be a major pedestrian bridge crossing the Lougheed Highway. The station platform straddles this bridge.

The enclosure consists of overlapping glass panels providing protection from the weather, and also offering good visibility and a safe environment for skytrain patrons. This extensive

5

5, 6 & 8   Interior platform

    7   Night view from south access stairs

glazing makes it transparent by day and glowing by night. Structural components of this station are a combination of wood and steel, which have been custom designed to provide the elegant curved shape that is efficient and cost effective to build.

'The project tried to do a lot of things that few others even thought about ... I liked the expressiveness, and the idea that this was happening on a public transit building, a type with a notoriously gloomy history in Canada of being grimly utilitarian and without much redeeming architectural identity or character.'

(Beth Kapuster, Juror, Canadian Architect Awards of Excellence 2001)

6

7

8

9 Interior platform

10 View from north access stairs

11 View towards platform from stairs

Photography: Nic Lehoux

9

10

BRENTWOOD SKYTRAIN STATION

1

BURDA MEDIA PARK

2

3

1 The building defines the boundary of the company and the outskirts of Offenburg

2 Section through Burda Media Park. The production hall and the refurbishment of the Burda high-rise are still under construction

3 The Burda Media Park is interwoven with the typical water-meadow landscape

OFFENBURG, GERMANY | ARCHITECT: INGENHOVEN OVERDIEK ARCHITEKTEN, DÜSSELDORF
STRUCTURAL ENGINEER: WERNER SOBEK INGENIEURE, STUTTGART | 2001

Journalism is chatting in the corridor' – this *bon mot* by Henry Nannen, one of Germany's most famous journalists, is valid even today; for journalism is no ordinary office work. The workstations for editors have to allow for informal exchanges. Creative editorial work needs room to move and an unconventional work structure. Hubert-Burda-Media is one of Germany's largest media groups. The majority of the more than 100 magazines which the group publishes are 'yellow press titles', entertainment magazines about 'the rich and famous'. As Burda-Media has moved on from dime store periodicals by launching journals like *Focus*, the client has become increasingly interested in architecture that reflects communication and journalism.

The head office of the holding company is located at the edge of the Black Forest, a fair distance from large conurbations in the region. At the foundation site near downtown Offenburg, the complex was developed in concert with the group's history. The original core quickly evolved into a hodgepodge of buildings.

Economic success overtook the building process. The Burda complex consists of an octagonal office building for the 'Burda Moden' magazines from the seventies, a 'functionalist box' by Egon Eiermann now protected as a heritage building, which has been renovated by Ingenhoven Overdiek Architekten, and a high-rise in the style of Ponti's Pirelli tower in Milan. It was to be given a new façade and a new roof edge. In addition, the

4

architects planned a new, round parking garage with an innovative visual and insulating screen composed of steel cables and round wood. The power station for the Burda printing plant has been equipped with a new roof skin reaching all the way to the ground. The 250-metre-long shed will be expanded with rooms for paper storage and the security plant.

The client, the city and the architect wanted to create a new image for Burda with construction work that adheres to a master plan for urban planning. The office building and the publishing house were built on the site of the former Kinzig Stadium. It is situated at the entrance to the city and is demarcated by a railroad embankment and the Kinzig River. The high profile location near the ICE tracks on the Frankfurt-to-Basle route was more important for the building's visual impact than integration with the city, as more people will see the building from passing trains than from the nearby road.

On this side the building is stunningly integrated into the charming meadow-studded landscape. The spread-out concept assigns a separate building to the individual editorial departments of the various publications, while keeping the circulation routes to a minimum. The street Am Kestendamm was slightly diverted, the bend in the road emphasised to follow the curve of the building. A small square was established in front of the main entrance.

The architecture of the Media Park can be interpreted as land art. Aside from the grand sculptural features, its unique quality lies in the communicative office workspaces, which are so important for a modern media enterprise. New office designs were developed for the editorial building. After all, the internal structure is just as important as the external image. The result is an organic and flexible officescape. The layout and combination of offices can be determined as required by moving the dividers. Individual offices, secretarial offices with waiting areas and conference rooms, even open decks, open-plan, combination and group offices can be set up throughout the building. The internal structure can vary from wing to wing and each section in turn is open to variation. This flexibility is an essential requirement because of the changing magazine titles and shifts in editorial responsibilities.

The building plays a large role in the employees' lives because they often work for long hours in their offices. Accordingly, the environment has to be experiential and should provide the workers with the feeling of being at home in their space. The architects conceived the office building as a living space and emphasised this quality at every workstation.

5

7

4   Along the drive-up side all fingers are connected
5   New Work Spirit – rapid flow of information between editors
    and staff
6   The building storeys are staggered like terraces
7   The façades are clad with untreated Canadian Oregon pine

6

8

8 The gardens are landscaped with lawns and fruit trees typical of the region

9 The building defines the boundary of the company and the outskirts of Offenburg

10 The gently curved roofs are the most distinctive characteristic of the complex

Photography: H. G. Esch, Hennef / Ingenhoven Overdiek Architekten, Düsseldorf

9

10

1

CAROUSEL PAVILION

2

1　A crisp openable glass box with wide-reaching roof shade is detailed to protect the carousel yet provide optimum transparency and legibility

2　Views from within maintain an uncompromised transparency and lightness that echo the carousel's framework

3　The Pavilion is the keystone of the new waterfront development

3

GEELONG, VICTORIA, AUSTRALIA │ ARCHITECT: McGLASHAN EVERIST PTY LTD
STRUCTURAL ENGINEER: PETER PLACZEK │ 2000

Historically housed in open-sided pavilions with high spreading roofs that provided shade, 19th-century carousels were attractions that encouraged social gathering and pause for refreshment. As part of the Waterfront Geelong redevelopment project the City of Greater Geelong wanted a modern Carousel Pavilion to provide a family-based seaside attraction and an historically significant focal point for Geelong's waterfront.

Flanking the east side of the new harbour on the Geelong waterfront, the Carousel Pavilion was required to decoratively showcase and provide security for a restored 36-horse carousel, a restored steam engine to drive the carousel, a band organ from the era and a period-style ticket box. Without landscape to moderate winds reaching across Corio Bay, the structure needed to be robust without overpowering the carousel. Transparency with shade for ultraviolet protection and permeability for those in the adjacent park or strolling the Bay Walk were required in an exposed location on the water's edge. Set slightly above sea level to seamlessly link the harbour promenade and the adjacent park, the pavilion can be viewed from above, when approaching downhill from the city, and from across the harbour so all surfaces are seen.

The Carousel Pavilion's form combines a transparent and permeable glass box with a bosk of six galvanised steel tree

4

4   The glass and steel framing provide a consistent grid
    counterpointed by the diagonal main steel frames

5   Western elevation reveals structural tracery that provides an X-
    ray with lyrical quality

6   An economy of means and budget proves no obstacle to an
    expression of elegant simplicity mirrored in Corio Bay

7   In the evening the carousel and the Pavilion glow enticingly

Photography: Peter Hyatt

forms, which branch to support a quilted roof of intersecting vaults. Inherently stable, the expressed steel structure was refined with 3D computer modelling to generate the most efficient framework and all members are at their minimum possible size. Diagonal main branches cantilever beyond the enclosure and are clad with expanded mesh to provide shade and control wind uplift. Walls are set along the length of the vault segments for simple glazed infill. The resultant dramatic roof form signals and attracts from afar as it shelters the transparent walls below.

The Carousel itself is 10 metres in diameter and approximately 6 metres tall, and consequently the building is substantial in size. To control scale for pedestrian approach and to provide a

second layer of shade and shelter a lower horizontal roof extends beyond the steel columns.

Large sliding steel and glass doors open the sides of the lower pavilion to the promenade and louvre panels and roof ventilators provide controlled natural ventilation. The honed concrete floor slab and services enclosure extend the existing hard landscape palette of the waterfront and a spaced boardwalk around the Pavilion acts as a drainage sump to avoid flooding when wave amplification in severe storm activity breaches the sea wall.

A lean project budget demanded a disciplined response and the building is evidence that a project founded on economy of materials can produce a spectacular result.

5

6

7

1

CELLULAR OPERATIONS HEADQUARTERS

2

1 Reception desk doubles as a coffee bar
2 Glazed wall drains onto Caledonian boulders
3 North-facing two-storey galleried break-out space

3

HILLMEAD, SWINDON, UNITED KINGDOM | ARCHITECT: RICHARD HYWEL EVANS ARCHITECTURE & DESIGN LTD.
STRUCTURAL ENGINEER: BURO HAPPOLD | 2000

Call Centres are losing their reputations as the pariahs of the building world, banished to distant orbits in undeserving northern British towns. However, as employment in these call centres increases, it has been necessary to take drastic measures to retain their understandably fickle staff.

The design for Cellular Operations Headquarters explodes conventional shed design, creating a great bulbous glass extension, blossoming out of a crisply detailed Miesian box, and supported on slim steel tubular columns. 'We set out to design a flexible office,' says Richard Hywel Evans, pointing out that the 4,500-square-metre column-free space provides vital flexibility – paramount in a call centre environment.

Swiftly dubbed the 'glass zeppelin' by the local press, the final product is more submarine than dirigible. Service and plant are located on the third storey, behind an elegantly louvred 'conning tower', looking out across the main two-storey workspace.

Behind the service area, which also houses the perspex and stud-lined lifts, are the main conference rooms and offices. Here the floorplan has been allowed to break out of the grid, and rectilinear partitions are eschewed in favour of an organic approach that reflects the building's exterior.

The Miesian box remains largely unchanged, with large sections of its south-facing façade glazed in Okalux insulated glass, allowing daylight to penetrate with little solar gain.

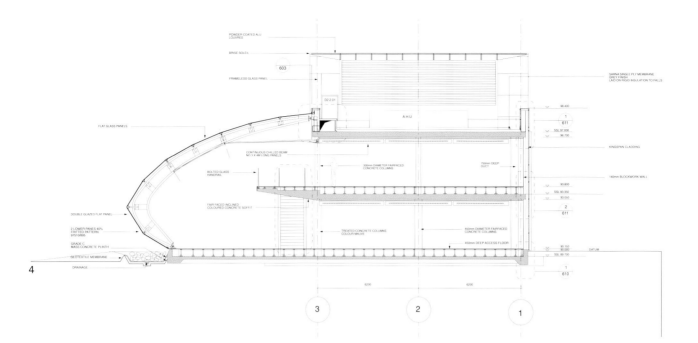

POWDER COATED AL'U LOUVRES

BRISE SOLEIL

603

FRAMELESS GLASS PANELS

SARNA SINGLE PLY MEMBRANE GREY FINISH LAID ON RIGID INSULATION TO FALLS

D2 2.01

A.H.U

98.400

1

611

SSL 97.000

96.730

KINGSPAN CLADDING

FLAT GLASS PANELS

CONTINUOUS CHILLED BEAM NO.1 X 4M LONG PANELS

300mm DIAMETER FAIRFACED CONCRETE COLUMNS

750mm DEEP DUCT

140mm BLOCKWORK WALL

BOLTED GLASS HANDRAIL

93.800

SSL 93.300

93.050

2

611

DOUBLE GLAZED FLAT PANEL

FAIR FACED INCLINED COLOURED CONCRETE SOFFIT

2 LOWER PANES 40% FRITTED PATTERN 975/0/805

GRADE C MASS CONCRETE PLINTH

TREATED CONCRETE COLUMNS COLOUR MAUVE

450mm DIAMETER FAIRFACED CONCRETE COLUMNS

450mm DEEP ACCESS FLOOR

90.150

90.000

DATUM

GEOTEXTILE MEMBRANE

SSL 89.700

4

DRAINAGE

1

610

8200   8200

3   2   1

5

6

Ronchamp-style windows have been 'punched' in this two-storey façade to provide visual interest. Naturally the building is wired for the latest IT, and all systems feed into a central 'brain', a glass-walled room at the heart of the building.

The internal staircase, which snakes up the side of this room, is an organic delight of poured concrete and underlit lozenge-shaped glass treads.

But it is the glazed extension that sets the Cellular Operations Headquarters apart from the herd.

In the best modernist tradition, the curved façade is not, of course, for show. As well as allowing precious daylight deep into the building ('You can't overvalue natural daylight,' says Evans), it functions as the key element in a simple ventilation system, drawing cool air off the adjoining lake, which is then dispersed through a network of vents running through the floor to the south of the building. A minimum of mechanical cooling and chilled beams provide backup, and the great curved façade sets up an efficient stack system within the building.

The centre's green credentials are highlighted by its relationship with the landscape, mediated by a sea of polished Caledonian boulders scattered about the upstand on the north façade, which are sculpturally uplit by concealed lighting.

Cellular Operations Headquarters is a delightful spin on a building type that has been shunned by aesthetics – a chance meeting between a decorated shed and a dramatic atrium.

The attention to detail has elevated what could so easily be a mundane building into a welcome diversion. Even the external electricity substation is cedar-clad and incorporates a seat, and the smokers' area is literally located behind the bike sheds.

The client's passion for the project is a welcome break from the traditionally antagonistic architect/client relationship, while the building's form aptly expresses the need for a humanistic, and occasionally humorous, approach to unstimulating work environments. The curved façade, expressive high-tech meets international style serenity, is an outpouring of humanity; a building in tune with its occupants.

7

8

9

4   Section through two-storey office
5   Two-storey steel structure sits on
    precast concrete ribs
6   View across the cooling lake
7   Hand-beaten aluminium reception desk
8   Themed bathrooms
9   Site plan

10

11

10 Precast concrete 'spine' staircase

11 Special spiders accommodate angle changes

12 Solar-controlled break-out space

Photography: John Ian Macleen © Richard Hywel Evans Architecture & Design Ltd.

12

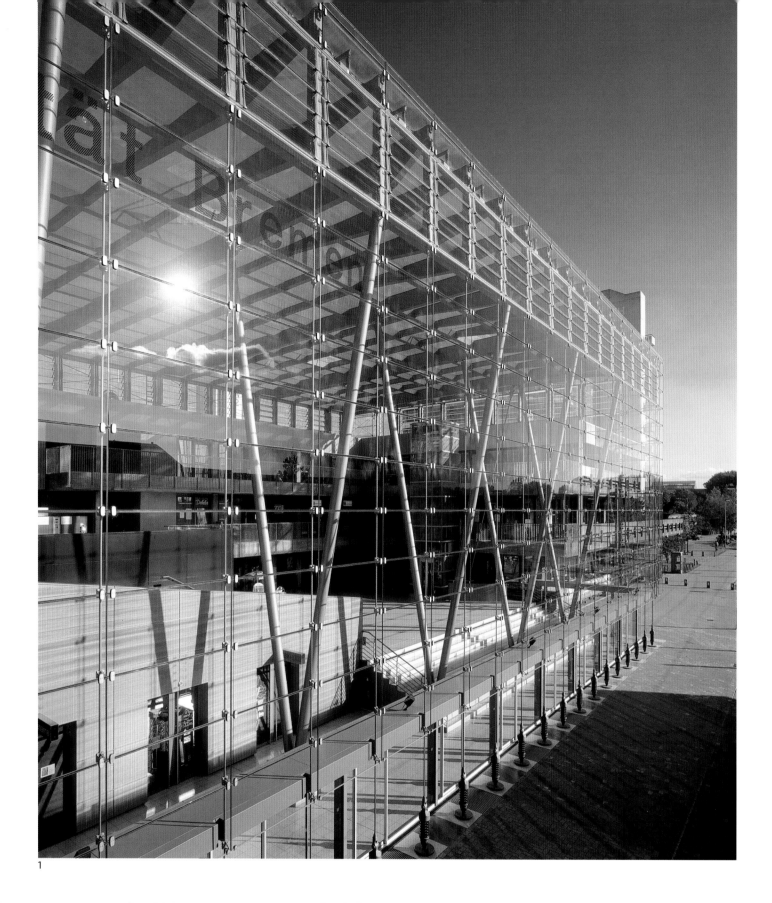

1

CENTRAL FOYER OF BREMEN UNIVERSITY

2

1 Façade on the university street
2 The lobby seen from outside

BREMEN, GERMANY | ARCHITECT: JAN STÖRMER ARCHITEKTEN
STRUCTURAL DESIGN: WERNER SOBEK INGENIEURE | 2000

The central foyer of Bremen University has been roofed with a filigree-like steel/glass structure. All four elevations and the entire roof area of the entrance hall are glazed. The hall, which adjoins existing buildings on two sides, is 15 metres high and has plan dimensions of 22 by 43.5 metres. The roof support structure is carried by six vee-supports in the foyer area and a further six supports on the existing building.

The necessary stiffening of the system is achieved by stabilising the outer two vee-supports by means of cables and by cross-bracing the pivoted columns. The elevations of the hall feature 39 vertical and equally spaced steel cables running between the edge of the roof and ground level; these are the only primary load-bearing elements of the façade. The cables are spaced approximately on 1.8-metre centres. They carry the mounting clamps for the glazing units and are mounted at the base by means of tilt and stay spring bearings. Under gale force wind loads this cable-supported façade is capable of being safely deflected from its flat state by up to 35 centimetres. This façade, which is solely formed by vertically tensioned cables, is the first of its type.

The glazing of the façade consists of 10- or 12-millimetre-thick standard safety glass panels (measuring approximately 1.8 by 0.9 metres), which are clamped at four points. The glass louvres below the attic provide ventilation and act as fume

3

4

extractors. The corner structure comprising tubes and cross braces is suspended from the roof structure. The areas of transition between the flexible and moving façade and the rigid corner structures on existing buildings, were realised by means of glass fins. In this way the façade can move freely along a defined transition zone without creating open joints.

The roof skin consists of walk-on glass panels (6-millimetre standard safety glass/a layer of printed foil/2 by 8 millimetre partially prestressed glass). Five hologram panels arranged in the plane of the roof intensify the daylight entering the hall. At night they are illuminated from outside and, together with the printed glazing of the roof, form a suspended brilliantly bright panel.

3   Tip springs seen from the boulevard

4   The stay springs along the entrance front

5   Rigid glass corner

6   Hall joining the existing building

7   Indoor view of the lobby with footing of the V-columns on a concrete base

Photography: Andreas Keller

5

6

7

CENTRAL FOYER OF BREMEN UNIVERSITY

1

THE CHRIST PAVILION

1 The enlightened Christ Pavilion in the Volkenroda monastery
2 Aerial photograph of Volkenroda
3 The access portals
4 View into the cloister

HANOVER, GERMANY │ ARCHITECT: GMP – ARCHITEKTEN VON GERKAN, MARG UND PARTNER
STRUCTURAL ENGINEER: BINNEWIES │ 2000

The Pavilion of Christian religions, a combined contribution of the Catholic and Protestant Churches for the EXPO 2000, is intended to be a contemplative counterpart to the vanity fair with architectural highlights: simple in structure, reduced to a few materials, precise in detail, unmistakable in its appearance and spatial atmosphere. The architecture of the Pavilion is restricted to the clear presentation of the modular construction and its details.

The surrounding cloister, 4 metres wide and 6.8 metres high, frames the overall complex and simultaneously functions as an exhibitions space. In the north the cloister comprises a voluminous hall 21 square metres and 18 metres high, with its roof supported by nine slender cross-formed steel columns. Lighting and strong verticality grant the hall its dignity and solemnity.

Spatial 'enclaves' are located in the transmission between 'Christ Hall' and the cloister as 'Rooms of Silence', where themes of Christianity and the Church are communicated to the visitor in a semantic interpretation. Staircases lead to the underground 'crypt'. The walls are freely contoured with fair-faced concrete and three of the large cross-formed steel columns are continued through from the expansive ceiling.

5

5 Access portals viewed from the Christ Hall

6 The glass-marble façade at night

7 Nine 18-metre-high steel columns support the roof
   in the Christ Hall

Photography: Jürgen Schmidt; Klaus Frahm; Gerhard Aumer (aerial view)

6

The spatial atmosphere of all areas is created by a modulation of light. The 'Christ Hall' receives light from top-lights centrally located above the column heads, emphasising the vertical quality of the slender columns. The surrounding surfaces of thinly cut marble laminated with glass form a light-transmissive envelope, its lively colours creating a spatial atmosphere. In contrast to this the lighting emphasis is in the 'crypt'.

The surrounding 'cloister' is equipped with a double glass façade, used as large-scale showcases. The space between is filled with materials of various origins: from nature with coal, rush, bamboo, wood strips, poppyheads, feathers and so on. From technology with toothed wheels, tea-strainers, hoses, lighters, one-way syringes. Depending on the filling the walls are more or less translucent, also partially transparent; consequently the light atmosphere is modified and varies dramatically along the cloister.

The complete complex with the exception of the crypt, the colonnade and the water basin was disassembled after the EXPO world exhibition and resembled in the cloister grounds of Volkenroda in 2001.

In this place, the Jesus confraternity works on the reconstruction of the oldest maintained Cistercian cloister in Germany.

THE CHRIST PAVILION

1

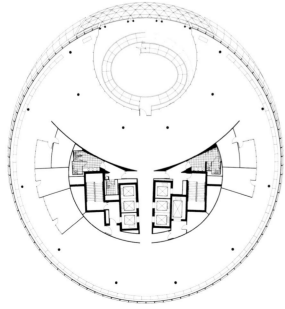

2

1 Interior view of ramp from below
2 Level 03 plan
3 Long section
4 General view with Tower Bridge in the background

CITY HALL

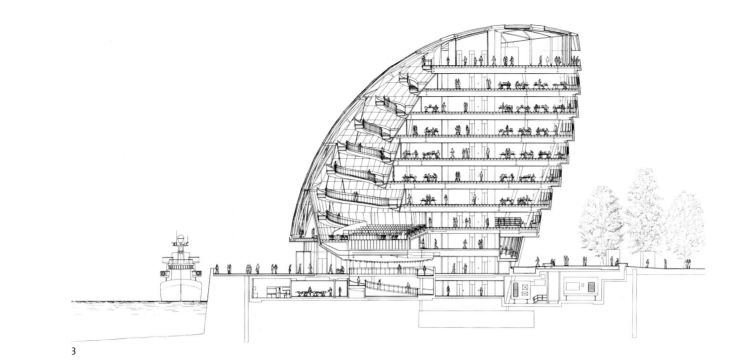

3

4

LONDON, UNITED KINGDOM | ARCHITECT: FOSTER AND PARTNERS
STRUCTURAL ENGINEER: ARUP | 2002

City Hall has been designed as a model of democracy, accessibility and sustainability. It houses the assembly chamber for the 25 elected members of the London Assembly and the offices of the Mayor and 500 staff of the Greater London Authority. It is a highly public building, bringing visitors into close proximity with the workings of the democratic process. The building is set within the new More London development on the south bank of the Thames, bringing a rich mix of office buildings, shops, cafés and landscaped public spaces to a section of the riverside that has remained underdeveloped for decades.

More than half of the total site area is given over to public space, including two large piazzas equivalent in size to Leicester Square and Piccadilly Circus. A new streetscape creates dramatic vistas of landmarks such as HMS Belfast and the Tower of London. An underground road, which gives common access to a service infrastructure shared by all the new buildings, has enabled the entire site to be kept completely free of vehicles. This has facilitated the creation of a new, completely pedestrianised public realm along the riverside, which will be accessible 24 hours a day.

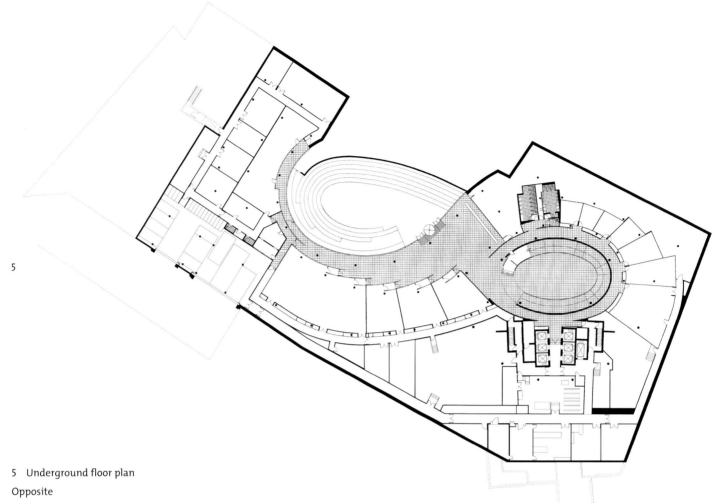

5

5   Underground floor plan

Opposite

   Interior view at bottom of the ramp

The public may enter the building either at the ground level reception or through a large sunken amphitheatre, which leads to a public café at lower ground level. Paved in high-quality blue limestone, the amphitheatre provides a space for outdoor events. Beyond the café is an elliptical exhibition space directly below the assembly chamber. Daylight is reflected into this space by the ceiling's pattern of concentric ellipses of mirror-polished stainless steel. From this space a half-kilometre-long, gently rising public ramp coils through all 10 storeys to the top of the building. At the level of the assembly chamber is a viewing gallery allowing the public dramatic views over the river to the Tower of London through the triangulated glass façade.

After the second level the ramp emerges inside the chamber and continues the rest of its rise directly above the heads of the elected politicians. Each step of the ramp offers new and surprising views of London and glimpses into the offices of the GLA staff. The ramp leads past the Mayor's Office to a public space at the top of the building known as 'London's Living Room'. This daylit space can be used for exhibitions and functions for up to 200 guests. Encircling it is an external viewing terrace offering unparalleled views across London. The assembly chamber is also open to the public, with 250 seats for press and visitors, including provision for wheelchair users.

The building's orientation and form have been designed to save energy. Its shape is derived from a geometrically modified sphere, a form which contains the greatest volume with the least surface area. The glazed façade of the assembly chamber faces north to minimise the amount of direct sunlight falling on it and so minimising solar gain. The building leans back towards the south, where the floor-plates step inwards to provide natural shading for the offices beneath.

The building has a highly integrated system of environmental controls to minimise its energy use. The perimeter office spaces can be naturally ventilated by opening vents positioned below the windows. The building's cooling system utilises cold groundwater pumped up via boreholes from the water table and passed through chilled beams in the ceilings, avoiding the need for noisy and unsightly chillers on the roof. Analysis indicated that, as a result of the combination of these energy-saving devices, the annual energy consumption for the building's mechanical systems will be approximately a quarter of that of a typical high-specification air-conditioned office building.

Advanced computer modelling techniques and innovative construction techniques have been employed to achieve the geometry. Each of the glazing panels is unique in shape and size. They have been laser-cut with data supplied from the same computer model used to design the building, ensuring a high degree of accuracy. Many of the building elements, including floor tiles and rubber doormats, are made from recycled materials. Designed and built within only 30 months, the building was completed on time and on budget.

7

8

9

10

Photography: Nigel Young/Foster and Partners

11

1

FEDERAL MINISTRY FOR CONSUMER PROTECTION, FOOD AND AGRICULTURE (BMVEL)

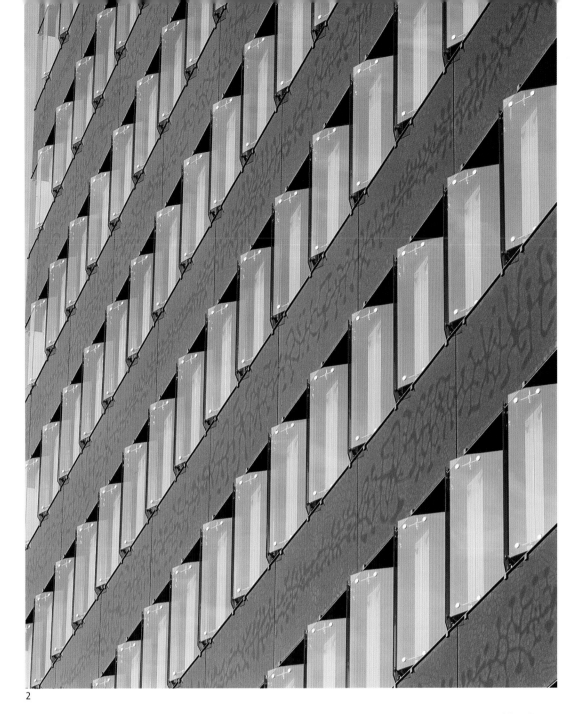

2

1 The double-leaf façade concept also serves to give the house a new identity

2 The external glass façade protects the internal wood-framed windows against exposure to wind and weather. Sensors linked to a climate control system automatically adjust the position of the tilt windows.

BONN, GERMANY | ARCHITECT: INGENHOVEN OVERDIEK ARCHITEKTEN, DÜSSELDORF
STRUCTURAL ENGINEER: SPI SCHÜSSLER PLAN, DÜSSELDORF | 2000

The Federal Ministry for Consumer Protection, Food and Agriculture (BMVEL) is one of the federal ministries that remained in the 'old capital Bonn' after the government moved to Berlin. The 13-storey administration building was created by Sep Ruf in 1968. It occupies the extensive grounds of a former barracks in Bonn-Duisdorf. The building featured a square ground plan and a plain perforated façade. Similar types of houses were erected at two other sites in Bonn. In the 'temporary federal capital Bonn', the area had been modified in a makeshift manner to accommodate the ministry requirements. In the 1960s and 1970s several new buildings were added and temporary structures demolished.

In 1997 the office was commissioned to undertake a thorough renovation of the building, which was severely compromised with toxic building substances. The planning task also called for the development of an innovative façade, the integration of additional conference rooms and a library in the adjacent single-storey building, as well as the conversion of a basement air-raid shelter. The architects decided not to renew the precast concrete façade of the high-rise, but to design a double-leaf façade with moveable panes and internal wood-framed windows. The double-leaf façade concept also serves to give the house a new identity. The unrelieved rhythm of the façade composed of closed parapets and columns left little room for play in terms of developing the design. The parapets

3

were preserved and the radiators behind it covered in new casements. This approach maintained the thermal storage capacity of the façade. Mechanical cooling and ventilation is unnecessary, despite the high degree of thermal radiation. The external stone cladding of the parapets was replaced with rear-ventilated glass components, which are flush with the external, adjustable skin.

The glass parapets were ornamented with a printed pattern of biomorphic forms designed by the artist Stefan Laskowski.

The structure of the 47-metre-high building remained virtually unchanged. The previously recessed ground floor was expanded, and this is the only area where the ground plan was modified. The interior spaces were in good condition: the wide corridors and exquisite materials, the light fixtures and skylights in the corridors are testament of the qualities of the original structure. The interior was therefore preserved, only asbestos-laden panelling was removed and replaced.

Ingenhoven Overdiek Architekten improved the proportions of the building by extending the façade beyond the height of the top floor. The glass skin stretches beyond the roofline and forms a new completion to the building. A roof garden was created above the 12th floor with a view over Bonn and the nearby Siebengebirge mountain chain.

This commission by the Federal Ministry marked the first occasion for the office to work with an existing high-rise building. The modification and redesign of the building is very pronounced. The aesthetics, functions and layers of the façade were newly defined. The quality of the interior was greatly improved by means of sensitive intervention into the building substance and now answers fully to the user requirements.

4

5

6

3 The building substance was modified on the ground floor and basement level
4 A cellar shelter and the registration and archive building were converted into conference rooms and a light-flooded library wing
5 The tilt windows of the new façade pivot around a point in front of the columns
6 Section

Photography: H. G. Esch, Hennef / Ingenhoven Overdiek Architekten, Düsseldorf

1

2

GRAMMAR SCHOOL MARKT INDERSDORF

3

1 Façade
2 View through the leisure hall
3 View from the leisure hall to the courtyard outside

MARKT INDERSDORF, GERMANY | ARCHITECT: ALLMANN SATTLER WAPPNER ARCHITEKTEN
STRUCTURAL ENGINEER: TISCHNER + PACHE INGENIEURBÜRO FÜR BAUSTATIK | 2002

The poetry of the place

The school lies at the edge of Markt Indersdorf, surrounded by a meadow landscape stretching to the nearby River Glonn. The meadows are frequently drenched with water, and the groundwater occasionally rises to the surface. The aim was to design a building that respects and brings out the poetry of this place while retaining its succinctness and identity precisely through the specific characteristics of the location, and the landscape was to be preserved as much as possible. The school therefore floats as an elevated rectangle above the meadows, and only the gymnasium and leisure hall are at ground level. This results in a clear, compact building that

leaves the site almost free for the school sport facilities and the school garden with its own expanse of water.

The school as part of the community

1,200 pupils attend the grammar school, all individuals in different age groups from different backgrounds and all with their own experiences. A great effort has been made to create for these individuals a place of identification and integration that arouses or reinforces their sense of community. The result, the elevated rectangle with the playground at its centre, appears as a suitable, simple-to-perceive symbol. The internal organisation is equally simple. In the western part of the two-storey tract are the classrooms, while the eastern part

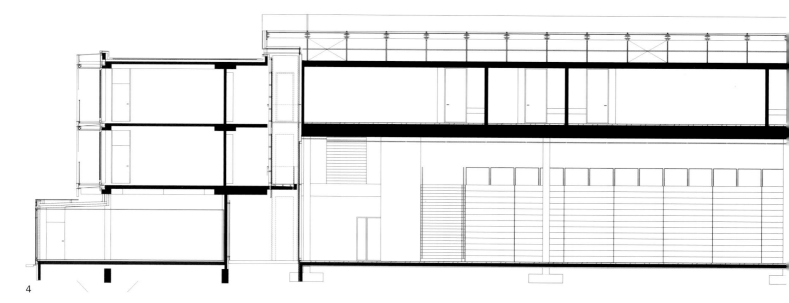

4

5

6

contains course rooms and specialist classes. The ground floor is taken up by teachers' rooms, administration and the gymnasium. Facing the courtyard are large staircases, partly in the open and partly within the leisure hall, encouraging communication, but also inviting to sit and relax. The geometric centre of the site is the tree-shaded playground courtyard. Irregularly placed deciduous trees contrast the hermetic ring form and, when mature, will dominate the view over the courtyard and interweave it with the surrounding landscape.

The different layers of the ring portray a progression through the various intensities of communication: from the place of individual learning, the classroom, through the naturally lit corridors with alternating views outwards and inwards, to the group communication areas such as the leisure hall and the playground courtyard. The diverse views, made possible by the hip-high wall concept, help pupils to get their orientation inside the school, atmospherically supported by the penetration of natural sunlight and the connection to the exterior or the larger rooms such as the gymnasium and the leisure hall.

Energy concept

The fundamental principle is to allow a maximum of natural daylight to enter the building. The massive internal construction

reduces maximum temperatures and creates a stable, comfortable room climate. The integrated gymnasium enables the use of alternative ventilation systems, thus avoiding great energy consumption and exploiting the warmth, and cold, of the ground. An earth duct system cools the inflowing air, which then flows out again through wide vents over the shed roof. The leisure hall profits from its situation in the same way: the massive floor, well isolated from the ground, is a composite of load-bearing ferrous concrete and industrial seamless flooring, and has a thermal storage effect. Heat protection in summer is provided by the internal location and by high-insulation windows and efficient ventilation. The massive, uncoated interior components serve as cool storage and also prevent overheating. The classrooms are protected by sunshades, but the low winter sun can penetrate deep into the rooms. The façade facing the inner courtyard is shaded in summer by the deciduous trees. In the winter, the sun's rays warm the corridor zones, unhindered by the leafless trees.

The declared aim is to use alternative concepts such as solar panels to heat water for showers, earth duct ventilation and air-cooling within the gymnasium, and thus avoid energy-intensive technologies and keep energy consumption to a minimum.

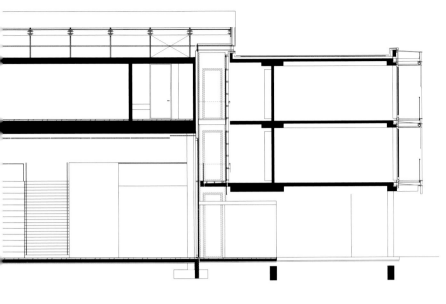

4   Section through classrooms, view to the leisure hall inside

5&7   View from the classrooms to the façade of the leisure hall

6   The gym

8   View from the landscape

Photography: Florian Holzherr, München (1,2,8), Stefan Müller-Naumann, München (3,5), Jens Passoth, Berlin (6,7)

7

8

HAUER KING HOUSE

2

3

4

1 Entrance
2 Rear ground floor looking out into the garden
3 Rear of house
4 First floor

Photography: Richard Davies

LONDON, UNITED KINGDOM | ARCHITECT: FUTURE SYSTEMS
STRUCTURAL ENGINEER: ANTHONY HUNT ASSOCIATES | 1992

The site is small, leafy and narrow in a conservation area in Cannonbury. It is unique in that it is wedged between the end of a listed Georgian terrace and the grander scale of a 19th-century listed pub. A structure on this site can therefore be seen as a pivot between the two buildings and yet be independent of them. Particular care was taken to preserve all the trees on this site; in order to avoid damaging the roots the result was small piled foundations. The design of the house takes advantage of the shading and privacy provided by the surrounding listed trees, creating an almost entire glass enclosure. The dominant cornice line of Douglas Road signals a change of glass on the front of the façade from the relative solidity of glass blocks, to a more fragile skin of clear frameless glazing sweeping to the ground at the back of the house. Inside a white ceramic tile is used throughout as a floor finish and is continued over the external terrace to break down the inside and outside. The back garden although small has an organic-shaped terrace and gently mounded grass to take the eye away from the enclosing garden walls.

HAUER KING HOUSE

1

HEADQUARTERS OF DEUTSCHE POST AG

2

1 Entrance area and base building
2 Base building at night

BONN, GERMANY | ARCHITECT: MURPHY/JAHN
STRUCTURAL DESIGN: WERNER SOBEK INGENIEURE | 2002

The design for the headquarters of the German Post Office in Bonn is based on an international competition. The design represents a new type of high-rise office building in terms of its integration into the townscape, its function, engineering and user-friendliness.

The foundations of the tower consist of a 3.5-metre-thick concrete raft and 60 piles up to 15 metres long. The five basement levels provide enough space for car parking and the utility installations for the building.

The tower, which in plan view is approximately 85 metres long by 40 metres wide, consists of two segments of a circle offset against each other; with its 41 storeys it reaches a height of

162 metres. Each circle segment has two concrete stiffening cores with a wall thickness of up to 80 centimetres, and 19 steel composite pivoted columns of diameters varying between 762 and 406 millimetres, depending on the altitude at which they are installed. The grade of concrete used for the cores varies over the height of the tower. The concrete cores are linked at five levels by means of diagonal stiffening crosses. Further stiffening is provided halfway up the building, on the technical installations level, by additional diagonal outriggers linking the cores with the external support columns.

Within the office areas the reinforced concrete ceilings are of coffered design and have a total height of 30 centimetres. They

3

are supported by a suspender beam running between the columns. The two halves of the building are linked at four levels by winter gardens, and at each level by glass-floored corridors. The roof area of the tower is enclosed by an 11-metre-high glass façade, which contains the roof garden and the penthouse, the latter being clad in a steel grid of double curvature.

The tower is enveloped by means of a second-skin façade that allows windows to be opened even on the upper levels and forms an integral part of the energy concept of the building, which is based on minimal energy inputs. Part of this concept is also the water cooling built into the reinforced concrete ceilings.

4

3 Glass-floored corridors

4 View over the Rhine from the sky garden

5 Sky garden area

6 Façade in the sky garden area, spanning over nine floors

5

HEADQUARTERS OF DEUTSCHE POST AG

Photography: Andreas Keller, Altdorf/Germany (1–3,7,8),

H.G. Esch, Hennef/Germany (4,5,6,9–13)

7

8

9

11

10

12

13

1

HERZ JESU KIRCHE
(CHURCH OF THE SACRED HEART)

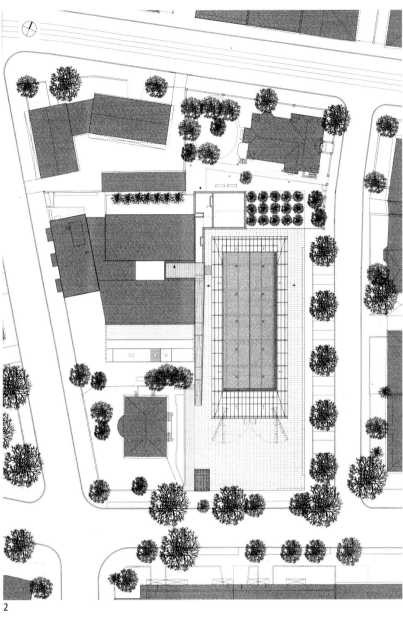

1 View from east; the inner wooden shell is visible from outer shell

2 Site plan

MUNICH, GERMANY │ ARCHITECT: ALLMANN SATTLER WAPPNER ARCHITEKTEN
STRUCTURAL ENGINEER: A. HAGL INGENIEURGESELLSCHAFT mbH │ 2000

George Sexton Associates' lighting design concept for Herz Jesu Kirche is a direct response to the architectural vocabulary implemented by Allmann Sattler Wappner. The lighting can be thought of as a system of layers, enhancing and enlightening the architecture while meeting the functional requirements of the church. Progression of surfaces and these surfaces' response to light and shadow determine the articulation of the design. The performance of the light can be experienced, but is not expressed, by hardware, emphasising the quality of the architectural materials, surfaces and forms.

We considered rendering the rich materials of the church a high priority for this project. The entire church is illuminated by tungsten halogen sources with Par56 wallwashers vertically illuminating the louvres and cross. Par56 adjustable fixtures provide, over the shoulder, horizontal illumination for the congregation and low voltage Par56 adjustable fixtures model the various objects. Specific functions of the church are accentuated and enhanced by the lighting and control systems. A twenty-zone preset dimming system controls every layer of light in the church. Due to the 14-metre ceiling height, low voltage Par56 adjustable fixtures accent the baptismal font for a christening ceremony. Two lamp types provide electrical illuminate for the worship space, low voltage and line voltage Par56. All of the fixtures are concealed and recessed in the ceiling to reduce glare and hardware appearance.

HERZ JESU KIRCHE (CHURCH OF THE SACRED HEART)

3

The concept was to have the natural daylight focused to the altar. This was achieved by positioning the louvres to angle direct sunlight towards the altar and respond to the movement of the sun. The spacing of the louvres creates sharp shadows at the entrance that gradually change to diffuse shadows at the altar. The appearance of the cross behind the altar gradually evolves throughout the day relative to the quantity of daylight to the electrical light. Par56 wallwashers are evenly spaced to illuminate the 14-metre-high cross, constructed of a polished metal mesh material. Low voltage Par56 adjustable fixtures accent the ambo and altar.

The compressed area under the choir box is expressed by a rough, low, concrete ceiling. In order to maintain a monolithic appearance, light comes from the surrounding areas to reinforce the feeling of compression. There is no lighting hardware in this concrete ceiling. The circulation route from the entrance to the choir box is highlighted with step lights. Low voltage step lights were selected for colour rendering consistency and physical size.

The church is experienced as a lantern and becomes a spiritual focal point for the community. The proper balance and amount of light is essential for the church's soft warm night-time identity. Par56 wallwashers were chosen to illuminate the outside surfaces of the wooden box. When the blue doors are open in the evening, an even wash of light illuminates the wooden box, however the altar in the background remains the focal point. Indirect light from the wooden box provides bounce light at the entrance while accent fixtures emphasise the altar. It is important to keep in mind the setting of the church and its integration into the neighbourhood. The entry plaza and tree-lined street areas provide a buffer zone, which soften and screen back the lighting from the adjacent residences.

4

3   Surrounding city reflected in the church façade

4   Open interior on a grand scale

5   View of altar

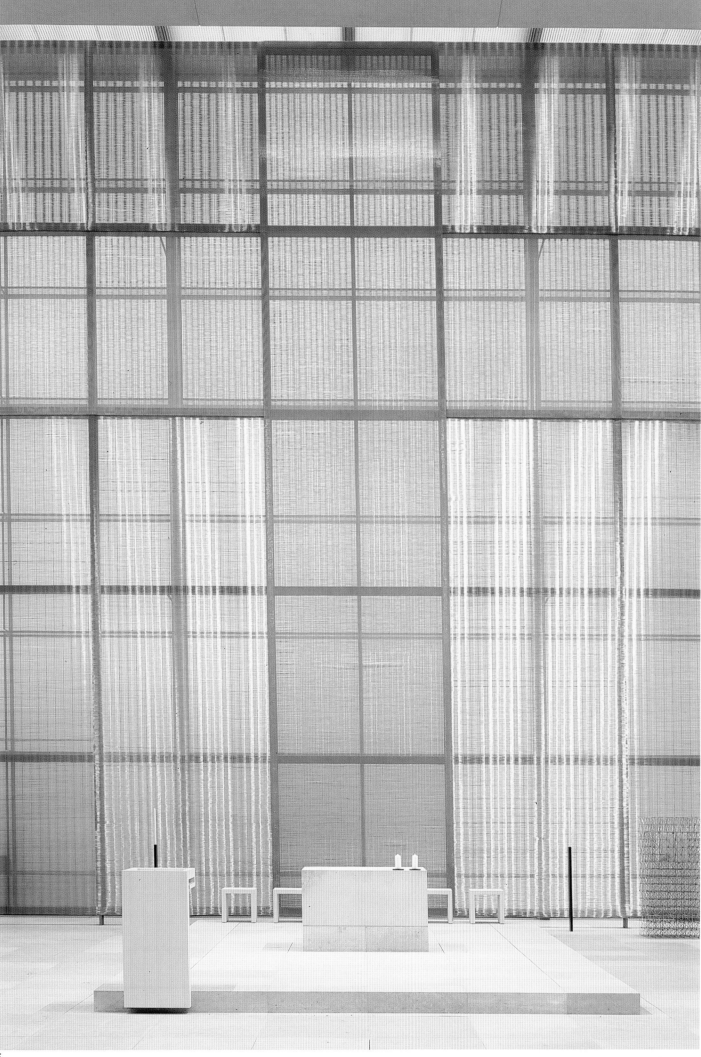

5

HERZ JESU KIRCHE (CHURCH OF THE SACRED HEART)

6

7

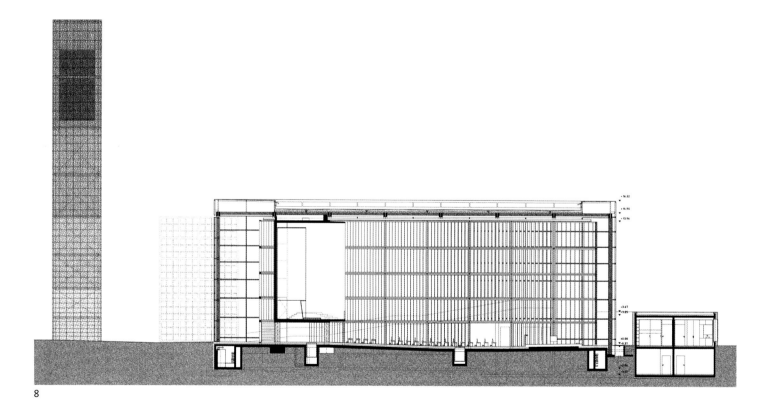

8

6,7 & 9 Views of the south portal from closed to wide open

8 Longitudinal section

10 View of altar

11 View between inner wooden shell and outer glass shell

Photography: Florian Holzherr, München (1,3–6), Jens Passoth, Berlin (10,11)

9

10

11

HERZ JESU KIRCHE (CHURCH OF THE SACRED HEART)

1

2

HOTEL HABITA

1 Building's day view from the street
2 Building's evening view from the street
3 Night view of the city from the roof terrace
4 Terrace jacuzzi

3

4

MEXICO CITY, MÉXICO | ARCHITECT: TALLER DE ENRIQUE NORTEN
ARQUITECTOS, SC (TEN ARQUITECTOS)
STRUCTURAL ENGINEER: COLINAS DE BUEN | 2000

On a fashionable commercial street lined with high-end stores and office buildings, the architects were commissioned to convert a five-storey apartment building into a 36-room boutique hotel. The new services and amenities, including a swimming pool, sauna, bar and restaurant, were added to the roof. Otherwise, only minor changes were made to the 1950s building, which was structurally and functionally sound.

The old structure gained an entirely new identity with a new skin, a frosted glass box of rectangular panels floating several feet from the original façade, creating an interstitial space. This

space acts as a climatic and acoustic buffer, regulating heat gain and loss and providing privacy for the hotel guests. The original balconies of the building are sandwiched between the new and old façades.

From a distance, the clean new façade appears to be an expressionless mask, but this impression is undone at closer range as the shadows of walkways become visible. Small, randomly distributed unfrosted squares and rectangles are the new façade's only adornment. These strategically transparent slots give each room controlled views to the city beyond, framing the desirable and screening out the unsightly. At night,

5

5&6 Lobby

7 Close-up of façade

the entire building appears as a lantern with a changing checkerboard pattern of illumination, varying as lights are switched on and off in individual rooms.

The rooms themselves, looking out to two planes of floor-to-ceiling glass (the inner transparent, the outer translucent), are suffused with natural light all day while maintaining complete privacy. The decor of the rooms mirrors the austerity of the outer enclosure – only a bed and a glass table occupy the space. This minimalist aesthetic heightens the experience of the otherwise compact rooms.

6

HOTEL HABITA

8

9

8   Roof-top pool at night

9   Night view from the roof-top pool

10 Day view from roof-top pool

Photography: Luis Gordoa (1,3,7–10), Undine Pröhl (2,4–6)

10

1

HOUSE IA

2

1 Exterior view
2 View of the lake from the living room

Valle de Bravo, México | Architect: Taller de Enrique Norten Arquitectos, SC (TEN Arquitectos)
Structural Engineer: Jaime Fragoso | 2000

The house was constructed on a sloping site with views to the lake and cliffs of Valle de Bravo. The site had stone wall remains covered by soil and gravel; these unfinished fragments were retained and a crystal prism was placed over them. The height of the stone wall remains dictated the levels of the new project.

A retaining wall forms the façade towards the street, and contains the lap pool. This wall also supports a wooden cube, which holds a water tank, set above the street.

The house is suspended in a fragile equilibrium between two bodies of water – the lap pool and the lake. The crystal volume, of Cartesian clarity and strict order, organises the programme

by means of its structure and holds the living room, dining room and main bedroom, all separated by a low volume that holds the service areas. The prism, simultaneously transparent and translucent, is placed over a stone basement that holds two bedrooms.

The glass-enclosed living room opens to the lake not only metaphorically, but the entire front slides, as does the façade, to the patio which turns, converting the terrace opening towards the lake and pool.

The wooden roof, supported by thin columns, appears to float over the interior walls without touching them, achieving spatial continuity. The inclined plane that responds to local urban

Photography: Jaime Navarro

4

3

5

guidelines is tilted to the north, opening itself to views and filtering sunlight. This wooden pergola extends the plane to the outside in the same way as the floor extends to the patio and outside, expanding the interior space and blurring the boundaries between the interior and exterior.

Materials have been kept to a minimum, using a neutral palette that enhances the exterior colours (lake, mountains and sky) and emphasises the changes in vegetation and landscape. The glazed envelope, besides showing a continuous view, creates a play of transparency and opacity that varies according to the different times of day, absorbing and reflecting the exterior colours.

Connections between materials reveal the construction system and its structural logic. The clarity and bluntness of these details form an integral part of the relationship between the materials and reinforce the bond between building and site.

6

7

8

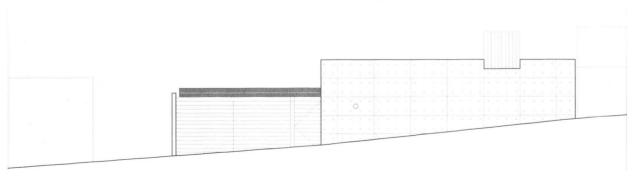

9

1

HOUSE IN WALES

2

1&2 Exterior

WALES, UNITED KINGDOM | ARCHITECT: FUTURE SYSTEMS
STRUCTURAL ENGINEER: TECHNIKER | 1994

Our objective has been to minimise the visual impact of the building and to site it in a way that makes the house appear a natural part of the landscape. The soft, organic form of the building is designed to melt into the rugged grass and gorse landscape, the roof and sides of the house being turfed with local vegetation. Views of the house are therefore only of grasses and the transparent glass walls outlined only by a slim stainless steel trim; an eye overlooking the sea. The surrounding landscape remains untouched with no visible boundary lines or designated garden area.

The simple plan is open and informal to reflect the lifestyle of the clients with the main seating area arranged around an open log fire. Two freestanding, brightly coloured, prefabricated pods house the bathroom and kitchen services without touching the roof in order that the space is perceived as a totality. A continuous block work retaining wall and steel ring beam support the roof, eliminating the need for internal columns. The roof is a plywood aerofoil construction covered with turf. The curved plywood underbelly creates a softness to the interior, complementing the organic form of the structure. It is an entirely electrically powered house with under-floor heating elements arranged around the perimeter walls.

3

Photography: Richard Davies

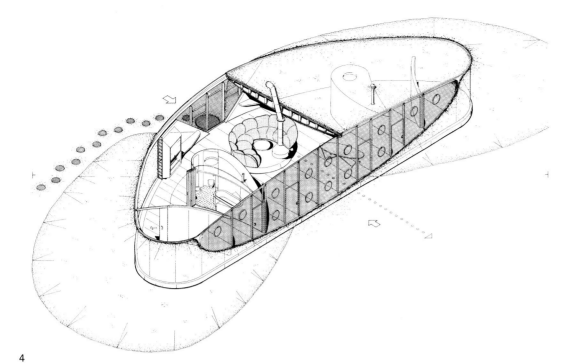

4

5

6

7

HOUSE R 128

2

1   Southwest elevation showing opened façade

2   North elevation at dusk

STUTTGART, GERMANY | ARCHITECT: WERNER SOBEK
PROJECT PLANNING: WERNER SOBEK INGENIEURE | 2000

This four-storey building which was erected 1999/2000 occupies a steep parcel of land on the edge of the bowl-shaped vale of Stuttgart. It was designed as a completely recyclable building that produces no emissions and is self-sufficient in terms of heating energy requirement. The completely glazed building has high quality triple glazing panels featuring a k-value of 0.4. Its design is modular. Because of its assembly by means of mortice-and-tenon joints and bolted joints, it cannot only be assembled and dismantled easily but is also completely recyclable. The electrical energy required for the energy concept and control engineering is produced by solar cells.

Access to the building is via a bridge leading to the top floor. This level accommodates the kitchen and dining area. The two levels below successively provide a living and sleeping area; the bottom level accommodates the nursery as well as the technical and utility installations. Each of the four levels is defined by a few pieces of furniture, repeating the concept of maximum transparency in the interior of the building as well.

The load-bearing structure of the building consists of a steel frame stiffened by diagonal members and erected on a reinforced concrete raft. The floors consist of heavy-section timber modules. All loadbearing and non-loadbearing elements as well as the façade are of modular design and assembled

3

4

5

3 Living/dining area

4 Stairs

5 Living area

6 Vertical access

7 Steel frame

8 Horizontal and vertical visual relationships and accents in the entrance hall

9 South–north elevation

Photography: Roland Halbe, Stuttgart/Germany

using easily separable methods of jointing. There is neither rendering or screeding, eliminating any compound materials which may be difficult or impossible to dispose of. For this reason there are no cables or pipes embedded in the walls. All supply or disposal systems as well as communication lines are housed in metal ducts which run along the façades and are built into the floor/ceiling structures.

To enable the house to be built as an emission-free zero-heating-energy house, an innovative computer-controlled energy concept was developed which can be checked by telephone or computer from any place on earth. The heat energy radiated into the building by the sun is absorbed by water-filled ceiling panels and transferred to a heat store from which the building is heated in the winter by reversing the heat exchanging process. In this mode the ceiling panels function as heat radiators; additional heating is not needed.

6

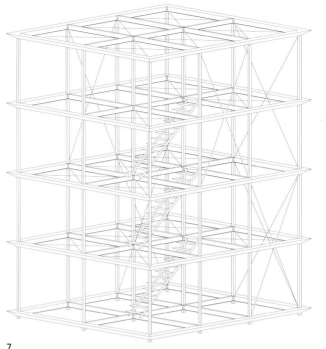

7

8

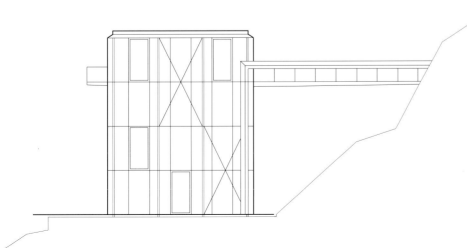

9

HOUSE R 128

1

2

HYDRAPIER

3

1 Overall night view

2 View of pavilion under canopy

3 View of waterfall entry

AMSTERDAM, THE NETHERLANDS | ARCHITECT: ASYMPTOTE: HANI RASHID +
LISE ANNE COUTURE
STRUCTURAL ENGINEER: INGENIEURSBURO, SMIT WESTERMAN | 2002

The award-winning HydraPier is a 1,200-square-metre structure that is located in proximity to Amsterdam's Schipol Airport and is inspired by both the technologies of flight and hydro-engineering. The pavilion consists of a 100-metre-long pier-like structure that projects onto an artificial lake. The controlled movement of water fuses with the architectural surfaces, creating a reflective and literally fluid surface. Water continuously flows down the two inclined planes of the roof and onto two glass walls located on either side of the entranceway. The pavilion, which originally functioned as a centrepiece of the 2002 Floriade Festival, remains a symbol of the Host City and continues to be used as a venue for exhibitions and special events.

In contrast to the frequent sight overhead of large body airplanes arriving and leaving Schipol airport and the endless streams of highway commuters, the HydraPier is sited within an artificially manufactured pastoral landscape. For much of the 19th century, this region lay beneath 5 metres of seawater and was reclaimed as land 150 years ago. The 19th-century engineered dams and pumping stations are still in existence today and are potent symbols of Holland's tenuous relation to the surrounding sea. The HydraPier is an architecture articulating the struggle between land and water, nature and technological artifice.

4

5

The HydraPier is a powerful architectural gesture on the shore of the Haarlemmermeer Bos, boasting an entrance bridge that allows visitors to enter through two cascading water-walls. There is an enclosed multimedia exhibition space surrounded by a large deck projecting out into the lake. The architecture of the pavilion itself consists of two large span inclined, metallic surfaces, on one side deformed to incorporate an impressive interior volume and at the other end an inverse deformation in the canopy accommodating an exterior pool above the entrance area. The planes become an architectural landscape that act in concert with natural and technological conditions that articulate this building's context.

4   View beneath canopy

5   Overall view of pavilion and canopy

6   View of water canopy

7   Entry

6

7

8

9

10

8   Curved glass enclosure

9   Interior view onto polder

10 Exterior view of pavilion

Photography: Christian Richters

1

ING Group Headquarters

2

1 West elevation

2 West–south elevation

AMSTERDAM, THE NETHERLANDS | ARCHITECT: MEYER EN VAN SCHOOTEN ARCHITECTEN BV
STRUCTURAL ENGINEER: ARONSOHN RAADGEVENDE INGENIEURS BV | 2002

The headquarter offices for the ING Group occupy a long, narrow site adjacent to the motorway ring around Amsterdam. The location is at the junction of two areas, the cosmopolitan high-rise of Zuidas and the green zone of De Nieuwe Meer. The building has been kept low on the green side, with the cantilevered auditorium as a projecting element, and rises towards the urban side.

The building rests on stilts measuring 9 to 12.5 metres in height, so that travellers on the motorway still have a glimpse of the area behind the building. This arrangement also means that none of the offices in the building have their view blocked by the motorway embankment. The entrance zone is ensconced between the stilts.

The new headquarters symbolises the banking and insurance conglomerate as a dynamic, fast-moving international network. Transparency, innovation, eco-friendliness and openness were the main starting points for the design. The building has an innovative interior environment control system. The double-skin façade allows natural ventilation of the offices without admitting traffic noise. An advanced air treatment system and the use of an aquifer under the building and a mechanical pumping system to provide cold/warm thermal storage make this building energy efficient.

3

The atmosphere of the interior is richly varied and features an alternation of open and sheltered spaces. Successive storeys intermingle and offer recurrent glimpses from one to another. Areas with a panoramic view, such as the restaurant, the large conference room and the auditorium, exist alongside introverted spaces. Atriums, loggias and gardens, both internal and external, are distributed through the building at various levels.

5

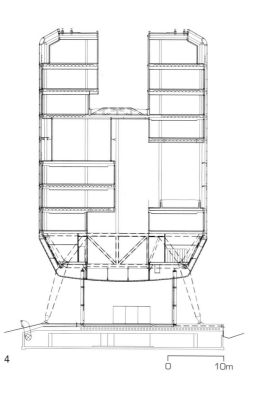

4

0   10m

6

7

3 Dining room, eighth floor

4 Cross section, axis 16A

5 Restaurant, sixth floor

6 View to reception, ground floor

7 Void with view from fourth to second floor and through glazed belly the bamboo garden on ground floor

8

8 Northwest elevation

9 Ground floor

10 South elevation; transition from auditorium (aluminium
cladding) to cascade (double skin glass facade)

Photography: Georges Fessy

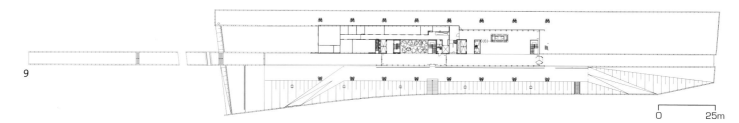

9

0   25m

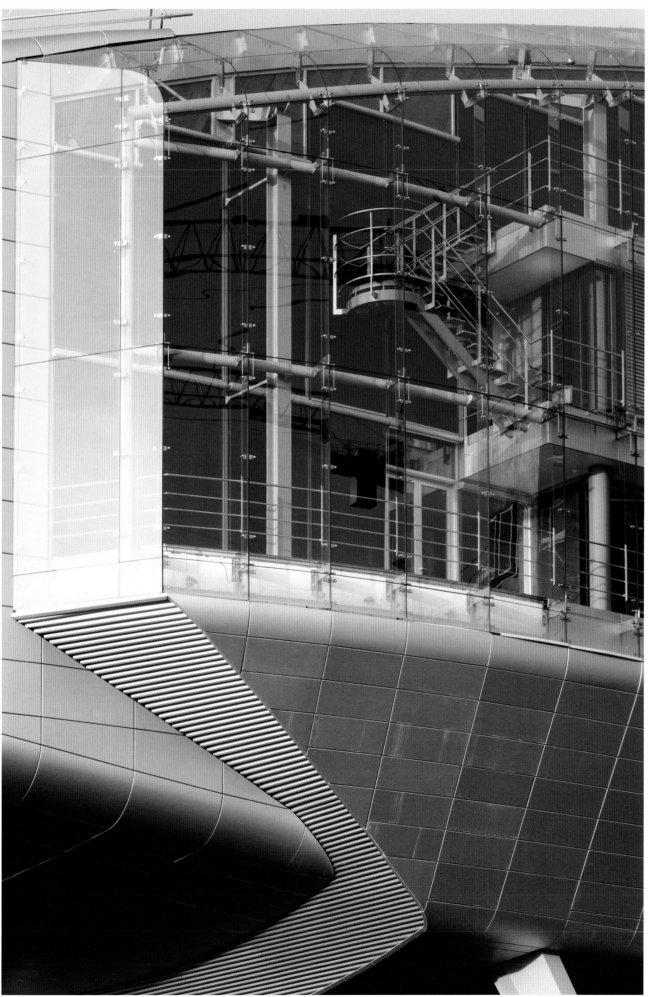

ING Group Headquarters

1

JENKINS ROBSON HOUSE

2

1   Existing terrace addition
2   Sitting area under roof garden

PADDINGTON, NEW SOUTH WALES, AUSTRALIA | ARCHITECT: ANDREW NOLAN
STRUCTURAL ENGINEER: PETER CHAN | 1999

The project is located on an elongated corner site (55 x 10 metres) in an 'intruded' part of a conservation zone in Paddington, Sydney. The Victorian three-storey terrace was built (circa 1878) by a builder for his family and a 1980s' addition effectively 'smothered' the original ground floor rooms. Views from the upper floors were dominated by a large expanse of roofing. The site is adjacent to four-storey flat buildings to the north, has several awkward level changes and no notable outlook.

The design is a direct solution to the problems of the site: namely to provide an outlook where previously there was none; to provide private indoor and outdoor spaces; to deal in a fluent way with the awkward level changes of the lot; to rationalise car access and parking; to marry in an uncompromising way old and new; to fit in a direct and simple way with the heritage surroundings; and beyond these physical considerations to provide shelter in the psychological sense – to create a private place despite its urban context to refresh the mind and spirit.

The 1980s' work was demolished and the original house allowed to 'breathe'. The addition is designed as a series of stepped indoor and outdoor spaces following the slope of the site and is connected to the existing building by a landscaped passage forming a courtyard garden between old and new. It is designed with a 1-metre level change from the existing ground

3

floor level, which conceals the new space from flat buildings to the north and reduces the scale and visibility of the structure from the existing house. The space is 'sunk' into the landscape with the kitchen counter tops flush with the courtyard and pool. Each level of the existing house has an outlook to the new gardens, eliminating visible roofs.

Circular operable skylights through the roof garden can be rotated to adjust natural ventilation. Stormwater is stored underground in an old swimming pool at the rear of the site and recycled for irrigation.

An aim of the project is that the character of the new space is neither subordinate to the existing traditional fabric nor dominates it. Nature and trying to create a sense of the infinite with the architecture itself are keys to this balance.

4

5

6

3 Living room terrace garden
4 Living room detail
5 Courtyard garden plus kitchen
6 Courtyard plus addition from terrace house
7 Passage to addition
8 Roof gardens

7

8

JENKINS ROBSON HOUSE

9

10

11

Photography: Peter Hyatt

12

1

KOEHLER HOUSE

2

1 Living Area
2 View from north end

NEW BRUNSWICK, CANADA | ARCHITECT: JULIE SNOW ARCHITECT INC.
STRUCTURAL ENGINEER: CAMPBELL COMEAU ENGINEERING, INC | 2000

This retreat house is located on New Brunswick's Bay of Fundy, with views of the expansive ocean and rugged coastline. Stunningly beautiful, this very exposed site is also subject to violent extremes of weather. Consequently, the house needed to offer protection without compromising the experience of this intense landscape. A stone wall, which contains the fireplace and storage, anchors the structure to the rocky terrain. Tethered to this masonry core are overlapping planes that cantilever above the outcropping as it slopes down to the sea.

Offsetting the spatial volumes of the residence offers a surprising variety of spaces within and around this small structure. The double height space created by the volumes' overlap forms the main living area. An adjacent, informal dining area and covered deck on the lower level are minimally separated from the living area by a pair of low kitchen counters. The other side of the central volume provides for a master suite above and guest room below. A roof deck, master bedroom terrace and a cascade of broad, south-facing steps extend the interior living spaces into the landscape.

3

4

5

The home's extensive glazing resists the caustic salt-air environment and powerful storms of this region. Resisting lateral loads through stiffened floor plates allowed a minimum of interior walls. Sill and head frames are recessed to create the least obtrusive separation from the surrounding view. The slightest enclosure stands between the occupant and the dynamic coastal landscape.

3 Section

4 View from northwest

5 Steps from living area to site

6 View from south

7

7   Bridge from reading room to deck
8   View from bridge to living area
9   View from northeast

Photography: Steve Dunwell (5,8,9), Brian Vanden Brink (1,2,4,6,7)

8

9

1

THE LOWRY CENTRE

2

1 Entrance canopy and foyer at night
2 View of artworks gallery and adaptable theatre foyer across
   ship canal

SALFORD QUAYS, SALFORD, ENGLAND, UNITED KINGDOM | ARCHITECT:
MICHAEL WILFORD & PARTNERS, LONDON
STRUCTURAL ENGINEER: BURO HAPPOLD | 2000

The Lowry is a landmark millennium building located on the Manchester ship canal to house galleries for the City of Salford's Lowry collection and Lowry study centre, the Artworks Gallery, a 1,750-seat Lyric Theatre, 450-seat Adaptable Theatre, rehearsal and dressing rooms with full support space, together with bars, cafés and retail. The Lowry Centre is a cultural centre containing facilities for both the visual and performing arts. It is intended to be a landmark as well as an exciting, stimulating venue for recreation and education.

It is the focus of the redevelopment of Salford Quays, bordered by water on two sides and facing a new triangular public plaza. The plaza is a sheltered and lively venue for community activity and gathering together. There are three primary approaches to the Centre, including the new metro link terminus. A hotel and parking building enclose the remaining sides.

Waterside promenades and a public park provide leisurely pedestrian routes from the entrance to the Quays.

A two-storey foyer extends across the full width of the plaza frontage to provide clear and convenient access to all activities. It will be open throughout the day, as part of the urban realm.

The Lyric Theatre forms the heart of the building. Stairs and balconies within its outer enclosure provide direct access to all levels of the auditorium.

3

4

5

Pavilions on each side of the foyer accommodate entrances to the Children's Gallery and Lowry galleries above. Shops on either side of the entrance doors can be entered either from the plaza or foyer.

The Adaptable Theatre has a courtyard form to suit proscenium traverse, thrust and in-the-round performances. Its curved foyer has dramatic views across the ship canal. A roof-lit galleria with dramatic views into and beneath the Children's Gallery connects the theatre foyers. An internal promenade around the building links all activities and enables visitors to browse and enjoy facilities throughout the day.

The Lowry galleries are arranged enfilade with relaxation and views out of the building. Additional top-lit galleries are provided in the promenade providing a flexible suite of rooms of varying scale and ambience.

The Children's Gallery comprises a large linear volume with a stepped floor and an interconnected series of geometric forms containing interactive exhibits and audiovisual displays. School parties can, if required, enter and leave the gallery directly from the quayside.

The bar, café and restaurant, ranged along the southern side of the building, serve both theatres and in fine weather can extend out to quayside terraces overlooking the canal turning basin. Upper level bars on either side of the Lyric Theatre open on to roof terraces overlooking the plaza and quaysides.

As the workplace of a wide variety of people dependent on personal interaction, the layout of the building is intended to encourage a sense of artistic community. Rehearsal spaces are provided adjacent to the Lyric Theatre stage and above the Adaptable Theatre and an artists' lounge with roof garden is centrally located above the scenery store. The administration tower is crowned by an illuminated sign announcing current productions and registering the presence of the Lowry Centre on the Salford skyline.

The Lowry Centre comprises a unique assembly of forms and spaces that expresses the range of the building's significance from cultural symbol to intimate place of personal experience.

7

6

3   View across ship canal

4   Lowry galleries promenade

5   Night view across ship canal turning basin

6   Lyric Theatre interior

7   Foyer bar and artworks gallery

Photography: Richard Bryant

1

LYON AIRPORT STATION

2

1 View of the station from north
2 The hall looking south
3 View of the station from north (from 5–6 kilometres)
4 View of the station from west

3

4

SATOLAS, FRANCE │ ARCHITECT: SANTIAGO CALATRAVA S.A.
STRUCTURAL ENGINEER: SANTIAGO CALATRAVA │ 1994

As part of a drive to boost trade through improved transportation, the Rhone Alps Region and Lyon Chamber of Commerce and Industry (CCIL) organised a competition for the Lyon Airport Station, the terminus of a new rail connection between Lyon and the Saint-Exupéry Airport, in Satolas. The competition brief called for a building that would provide smooth passenger flow while creating an exciting and symbolic 'gateway to the region'.

The platform hall, on the project's lower level, spans a central enclosed caisson, which shields waiting passengers from the non-stop, high-speed trains (300 kilometres per hour) that run on two central tracks. The caisson's cover forms the walkway

of the platform hall: a longitudinal, arched concrete structure, 500 metres long, bridged at two points by a unifying, symmetrical road pattern. Access to the platforms is provided via concrete bridges, stairs, escalators and glass elevators. Four tracks serve the station – two on each side of the central walkway – and provision has been made for two further tracks outside the platform hall to serve 'Satorail', the future regional connection to Lyon.

A concrete vault of intersecting diagonal arches spans the platforms to create a lamella roof spanning 53 metres. The structure has been cast in situ, including recesses for light fittings. Through the use of a local white sand in the mix, the

5

concrete has a natural colour. Above the tracks, the matrix of this roof is open to the sky; above the platforms, it is either glazed or filled with prefabricated concrete slabs.

The glazed central hall, triangular in plan and spanning 120 metres, sweeps upwards towards a service concourse on the east side, which accommodates ticket offices, retail shops, restaurant facilities, a temporary exhibition space and access to the airport. This multilevel service block also houses the station master's office, the airport police and offices and technical areas for the SNCF and CCIL. The central hall is thus left free of visual obstructions. The service concourse is connected to the airport by a raised, 180-metre steel gallery, which in turn connects to a covered extension for pedestrian access to the parking garage, underground service area and elevators. Bus and taxi terminals are located to the west.

The dramatic form of the central hall's superstructure derives from one of Calatrava's sculptures: a balanced shape resembling a bird at the point of flight. The steel roof is composed of four converging arches with a curved, tapering, arched spine. The inner arches, which support the central spine, spring from a lintel placed across the elevator towers; the outer arches spring from two tapering concrete buttresses on each side of, and beyond, the eastern façade. A single, sculpted, V-shaped, concrete footing supports the arches at their point of convergence on the west. Glazed side screens fill the area between the central, concrete arches of the platform hall and the two outer steel spans of the concourse roof, stabilising the structure. The arches to either side of the central concourse also form the portals to the platforms. Floodlights are recessed into the upper, exterior surfaces of the portal arches, providing reflected illumination onto the concourse.

5   The hall looking north

6   The hall looking south

7   The walkway looking north

Photography: Paolo Rosselli

1

MAISON HERMÈS

1   View of the entrance zone
2   Night view
3   Roof terrace

2

3

TOKYO, JAPAN | ARCHITECT: RENZO PIANO BUILDING WORKSHOP
STRUCTURAL ENGINEER: OVE ARUP & PARTNERS | 2001

A thin and tall, yet elegant 11-storey building in a lively Tokyo area. With its earthquake-resistant glass brick façade, the Maison Hermès becomes the 'magic lantern' of the city at night.

French group Hermès chose the Ginza district, in the heart of Tokyo, for its Japanese headquarters, a 6,000-square-metre building consisting of shopping space, workshops, offices, exhibition and multimedia areas, topped by a French-style hanging garden. This project was both an aesthetical and technical challenge. How, in the architectural diversity of Tokyo, could a 'landmark' building be conceived that would comply with the strict anti-seismic standards in Japan? The idea of a 'magic lantern' lighting up in Ginza, like the ones traditionally hung at the doors of Japanese houses, soon made its way.

The 15-floor building is 45 metres long and 11 metres wide. Its façades are entirely made of 45 by 45 centimetre specially designed glass blocks, the result of an industrial development. These are the materials used to weave this 'glass veil', creating a continuous and luminous screen between the serenity of the inner spaces and the buzz of the city.

MAISON HERMÈS

4　View of glass façade
5　Detail view of glass blocks
6　10th-floor meeting room with roof garden beyond
7　Corners are composed of smaller glass bricks
8　Exhibition space on 8th floor features large reflecting pools

Photography: Michel Denancé

4

5

The twofold aspect of interior/exterior, the alternation between day and night, light and transparency leaves more to the imagination than can actually be seen, and gives a refinement to the façade. The atmosphere created imparts both a traditional and a technological character to the building.

The balance is also the key to the innovative anti-seismic system inspired by traditional Japanese temples that still stand despite frequent earthquakes. The backbone of this building is made up of a flexible steel structure, that is articulated at structurally strategic locations with visco-elastic dampers, from which cantilevered floors span to support the suspended glass block façades.

The entire building can move during an earthquake, according to predefined displacements, uniformly distributed all over the structural parts of the building. Each element of the construction absorbs its share of the movement due to it. In this way, not only the integrity of the structure is guaranteed, but also that of the numerous networks that entice the building as well as its water and air tightness.

At the centre of the building, a small, open square connects the street to the subway station two levels below, via a long escalator integrated into the project. A mobile sculpture by sculptor Susumu Shingu, overlooking this space from the entire height of the building, engages in a continuous play of light between the façade, the city and the sky.

7

6

8

MAISON HERMÈS

1

MINERAL BATH EXTENSION
AND RENOVATION

2

1 Bathers are shaded by louvred glass
2 Leafed glazing filters light and colour onto neutral surfaces

BAD ELSTER, GERMANY | ARCHITECT: BEHNISCH & PARTNER
STRUCTURAL ENGINEER: FISCHER + FRIEDRICH | 1999

The architect's comprehensive design sensitivity took the resort's setting and history into account. The resort is in a densely wooded area at the centre of an historic park that features promenades, extensive green areas, old trees and small lakes. Changes throughout its history incorporated diverse styles of architecture. Parts of the old complex were torn down; most technical parts were renewed and some parts had to be built from scratch. New buildings contain shielded and open baths, terraces, as well as reception and therapeutic areas.

The formal courtyard, with its pools, lounging areas and high-quality flooring, is the focal point of the complex. A glass and steel roof shoots out above it, supporting wonderfully bright, colourful and festive shutter forms. The array here makes a 21st-century statement without speaking over the original 19th-century commentary. The design encourages the dialectic between old and new, inside and outside and festivity and formality.

The architects saw the courtyard and its surrounding as a kind of stage production of old and new features. The architects reduced the new buildings to their essence, so they remain as stage props behind the provocative, colourful action happening under the multicolour proscenium arch.

3 Abstract art is designed in the pool
4 Glass is white on the upper sides (facing sky) and colour on lower sides (facing interior)
5 Formal courtyard is focal point of complex
6 Old forms contrast with new
7 New structure respects old

Photography: Christian Kandzia; Peter Blundell Jones

3

4

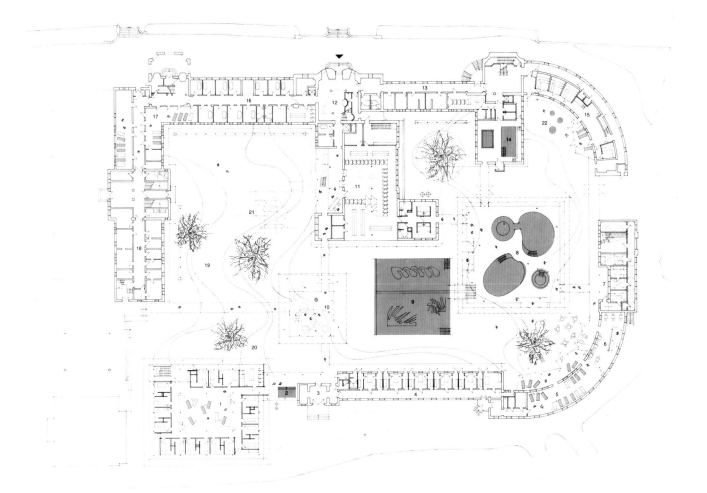

5

7

6

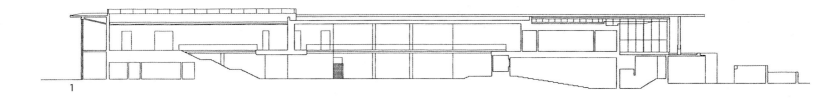

1

2

MODERN ART MUSEUM OF FORT WORTH

1 Longitudinal section
2 Evening view over the artificial pond. The structure floats on the water and looks like a lantern.
3 View of the museum from the terrace of the café
4 Overall view over the artificial pond

4

3

FORT WORTH, TEXAS, UNITED STATES OF AMERICA | ARCHITECT: TADAO ANDO ARCHITECT & ASSOCIATES | 2002

This museum of modern art was relocated and newly constructed in the city of Fort Worth, Texas. It is located on a 44,000-square-metre site across the road from the Kimbell Art Museum designed by Louis I. Kahn. The museum is conceived as 'An arbor for art', indicating that the whole of this extensive site is conceived of as an environment for the unhurried appreciation of art.

The building consists of rectangular concrete boxes in a parallel arrangement, each box being sheathed in a skin of glass. To the east there is a spacious water garden and a grove of trees, which shield the museum from a heavily travelled intersection and create a tranquil natural environment.

The structure uses glass and concrete, two of the representative materials of this century. Sheathed within their glass skins, the concrete parallelepipeds emphasise the transparency of the glass, while the glass softens the strong impression that would otherwise be created by the exposure of massive forms to the environment.

The material strength of concrete protects the priceless art works housed within the museum from the extremes of the local climate. The interior concrete boxes assure structural security and the exterior glass boxes ameliorate the direct influence of the external climate on the exhibition spaces.

5

6

Although the overall configuration of the complex is simple, various types of places and volumes are provided for the exhibition spaces, with further variety added by the use of several different natural lighting systems. The mediating spaces enclosed between glass and concrete walls are like the engawa of Japanese traditional architecture, belonging to both interior and exterior. They are utilised as integral parts of the exhibition spaces, as well as to stimulate the spirit of creation while incorporating the light, water and greenery of the surrounding environment.

The intention is to provide a truly open museum, one that will serve as a refreshing oasis in the midst of the severe local climate and an arbor of peace to stimulate the spirit of creativity.

5 Colonnade between the skin of the glass and concrete box, which contains the exhibition space

6 Main staircase leading to the exhibition hall. The art piece is 'Self-portrait' by Andy Warhol.

7 Concept sketch

8 Entrance hall

9 Two-storey-high space in the exhibition area

10 Exhibition space created by architectural concrete, which has an oval plan. The art piece is 'Book with Wings' by Anselm Kiefer.

Photography: Mitsuo Matsuoka

7

8

9

10

MODERN ART MUSEUM OF FORT WORTH

1

MOTOR SHOW STAND FOR AUDI AG

2

3

4

1 The loop is curved in plan and elevation, thereby evoking the desired enveloping effect

2 The curvatures resulted in a free-standing construction

3 The bays in a variety of sizes accommodated lounges, offices, conference rooms and catering areas

4 The primary loadbearing structure consists of screw-fitted steel tubes, which form a three-dimensional, rhomboidal grid that is stabilised by the double curvature in the plan and the single curvature in the elevation

Photography: H. G. Esch, Hennef / Ingenhoven Overdiek Architekten, Düsseldorf

FRANKFURT, GERMANY | ARCHITECT: INGENHOVEN OVERDIEK ARCHITEKTEN, DÜSSELDORF
STRUCTURAL DESIGN: WERNER SOBEK INGENIEURE, STUTTGART | 1999

The structure of the new motor show stands for AUDI AG, used for the first time at the IAA 1999 in Frankfurt, Germany, consists of a multiple-curve glass loop which is animated by the projection of coloured light and changing film sequences. The wall is 6 metres high and varies in length from 100 to 300 metres, depending on the size of the stand. The 4-millimetre-thick glass panes of satinised standard safety glass are held in a narrow-mesh cable net, which is mounted under tension in a grid structure consisting of curved stainless steel tubes that cross over each other.

The semitransparent envelope encloses the exhibition stand and divides it into an inner and an outer area. The vehicles are displayed inside the loop on a slightly inclined floor. The area outside the envelope is reserved for services, meeting rooms, a VIP lounge and so on. Various degrees of transparency create varying perspectives. The internal surfaces of the loop are used for the projection of films backed by simple sound collages. The prime objective is not the presentation of the product but the conveying of a total sensual experience.

Despite its size and complex structure the loop can be erected in a relatively short time. This is achieved by clever logistics and detail planning that is closely tailored to the sequence of assembly. The structure consists of few components that are assembled in stages, allowing the stand to be erected in separate phases.

The AUDI exhibition stands have received many design and architectural awards, among which is the 'Preis des Deutschen Stahlbaues'.

1 East entrance
2 Reading room
3 Children's space
4 West entrance

1

MULTIMEDIA LIBRARY (MEDIATHEQUE)

2

3

4

VENISSIEUX, FRANCE | ARCHITECT: DOMINIQUE PERRAULT ARCHITECTE
STRUCTURAL ENGINEER: GUY MORISSEAU | 2001

The Central Media Library in Vénissieux, a suburb of Lyon, is characterised by its box-like structure and gleaming panelled façades. The external walls are double-glazed, with folded and perforated aluminium panels set between the glass, giving a translucent, shimmering effect. The entrance to the building is dominated by the oversized lettering on the sliding doors.

Inside, all library functions are brought together on the ground floor. The children's reading and activities area occupies the north wing while the two older age groups share the south wing. The spaces are separated by a 50-seat auditorium, and

a lift to the three floors above and basement area below. Various spaces are further defined by the strategic placement of furniture, bookshelves and desks, creating a vibrant, open and informal space.

Materials used are solid and exposed – concrete columns, steel trusses, exposed ceiling ducts and wiring.

The ground floor area is encircled by a 3-metre-wide internal street that allows access to all areas from several points, and echoes the wide footpath that surrounds the exterior of the building.

MULTIMEDIA LIBRARY (MEDIATHEQUE)

5

6

Breaking the formal symmetry of the building is a three-storey box-like structure that sits slightly off-centre above the ground-level structure. This building houses the administrative offices, an independent entity yet well-connected to the activities of the mediatheque. Skylights in the roof bring daylight to the centre of this structure.

The economy of the programme is found in its simplicity. Its direct design approach, configured with economy and simple materials, convincingly relates to the wider intent of education and learning.

7

8

5   Gallery around the reading rooms

6   Gathering space for children

7&8   Façade details

Photography: Georges Fessy, André Morin

1

MUNICIPAL LIBRARY
(STADT-UND LANDESBIBLIOTHEK)

2

3

1 Overall night view pointing out the transparency of the conical library volume

2 View from northwest

3 Detail of the glass and steel structure characterising the library's shape

DORTMUND, GERMANY | ARCHITECT: MARIO BOTTA
GLASS/STEEL STRUCTURES: HELMUT FISCHER GMBH, KONSTRUKTIVER GLASBAU | 1999

'The design aims to consolidate the urban front of the city at the exit to the railway station. That is why the new building is divided into two distinct parts: a massive austere red stone linear volume re-establishing the walled front and a truncated glass cone, protruding from the alignment, to be used as the reading room and leisure facility.

The interest and tension in the design should arise from the contrast between the two elements and the varied handling of their materials.' (Mario Botta)

Libraries today lament a loss of identity linked not only to the introduction of new technologies but also to a 19th-century heritage that they have never been able to shed and that binds

them increasingly to the image of static container unsuitable for satisfying society's demands.

Botta's idea here is to stress the public dimension of the new building, so he divides the complex into two distinct parts. It is situated next to the railway station, and stands as a symbol of the city.

The layout develops as a rigid, linear body, almost a solid wall, and opposite, a transparent, truncated cone is the library's reading room.

The façade of the large tower volume is broken at regular intervals by slender vertical openings that contrast with the

4

5

4   Detail of the junction between the steel/glass structure and
    the stone wall

5   Interior of the library's reading room on the second floor

6   Detail of the steel structure supporting the glass curtain

7   Close view of the bowed façade shape with the horizontal
    window subdivision

Photography: Markus Steur

strong, solid image of the parallelepiped. The double-glazed
'skin' of the reading room is structured by a skeleton of steel
elements, like the tie-beams of a circus tent, that support by
means of tension the flat roofing surface.

The interior image allows a glimpse of the distribution of paths
on the two floors that house the reading rooms, consulting
rooms and computer rooms. Inside a network of vertical paths
links the different levels and suspended glass bridges join the
rooms with other spaces carved in the more solid linear body.

The contrast between the two volumes and the different
nuances of the materials create a very strong tension running
through the two distinct images. The entrance at the back of
the semicircular room stands at the centre of a covered path
that separates the two buildings. Proceeding upwards, the
levels of the circular-shaped building are progressively
recessed, so that a series of terraces allow a more uniform
diffusion of the light in the interiors. This also creates a net
separation between the library building and the rest of the
complex. The new Dortmund library site stands as a symbol for
the reconstruction of memory and the development of the
future, thus re-conquering its role as a point of reference in the
culture and traditions of man.

6

MUNICIPAL LIBRARY (STADT-UND LANDESBIBLIOTHEK)

1 Test match day
2 Restaurant
3 Media area
4 Isometric
5 NatWest Media Centre

Photography: Richard Davies

1

NATWEST MEDIA CENTRE

2

3

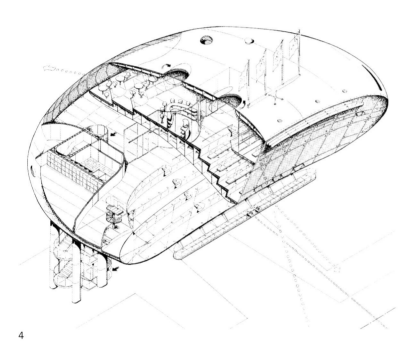

4

5

LORD'S, UNITED KINGDOM | ARCHITECT: FUTURE SYSTEMS
STRUCTURAL ENGINEER: OVE ARUP & PARTNERS | 1994

There exists at Lord's a tradition of patronage of innovative structures. The objective of the design has been to respect and savour the essential nature of Lord's while bringing to it a building that will herald the coming millennium and provide the most elegant and state-of-the-art media centre in the world. The NatWest Media Centre at Lord's is one of the most innovative buildings this century. It is the first all aluminium semi-monocoque building in the world. It represents a breakthrough, not just in the creation of a new three-dimensional aesthetic, but also in its method of construction. This building was built and fitted out not by the construction industry but by a boatyard, using the very latest advances in boat building technology. Raised 15 metres above the ground, the aerodynamic contours of the building reflect the sweep of the plan of the ground with the enclosing skin formed by a smooth, white, seamless shell. The west-facing glazing is inclined to avoid any glare or reflections while providing unobstructed views of the game for the world's media.

1

THE NEW 42ND STREET STUDIOS

2

NEW YORK, NEW YORK, UNITED STATES OF AMERICA | ARCHITECT:
PLATT BYARD DOVELL | LIGHTING: VORTEX LIGHTING
STRUCTURAL ENGINEER: ANASTOS ENGINEERING ASSOCIATES | 2000

The New 42nd Street Studios is a completely modern 11-storey creative 'factory' for the performing arts designed for The New 42nd Street, Inc., the non-profit developer of the historic theatres of the 42nd Street Development Project. Mid-block on the north side of 42nd Street between Times Square and Eighth Avenue, the 7,803.6-square-metre new building contains 12 rehearsal studios, two combined studio and reception halls, a 199-seat 'black box' experimental theatre – known as 'The Duke on 42nd Street' – and related administrative offices, dressing and locker rooms, storage and other support space for dance companies and other non-profit performing arts groups. At ground level the building incorporates retail space and the 42nd Street access to the lobby of the American Airlines Theatre on 43rd Street, formerly known as the Selwyn.

In place of the conventional illuminated signage called for by the 42nd Street Redevelopment Project, the building's façade is a collage of metal and glass, with sun-catching dichroic glass at the base, a 53.34-metre high-tech vertical LightPipe and an array of perforated metal blades presenting an infinitely variable display of coloured light projected from ranks of programmable theatrical fixtures. Behind the blades, the transparent glass of the building adds the animation of the lights of the studios and the actual movements of the dancers

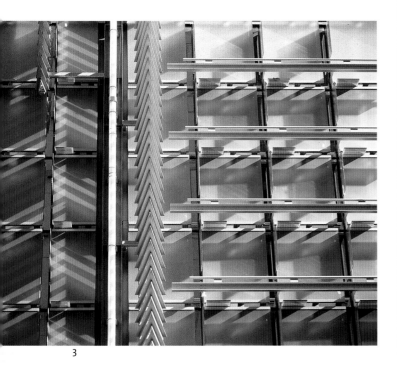

3

4

3   Feature wall

4   Entry canopy, LightPipe, sign armature

5   Performance rehearsal studio

at work and at the *barres*. Inside, the spirit of the collage pervades the building in inventive, colourful signage and graphics. Standing out from the hokey commercialism of its surroundings, the sensuous and engaging abstraction of the building strongly and appropriately announces 42nd Street's principal working venue for performing artists operating at the creative edge. At the same time, the building's inventive design explores and shows off for the first time some of the creative possibilities inherent in interpretations of the 'tacky' lighting associated with historic Times Square and vindicates the notion that the 'character' of Times Square was worth substantial efforts to preserve.

Winner of the 2002 AIA Honor Award for Architecture; 2001 New York State AIA Design Award; and 2001 New York Chapter AIA Design Award. Among other awards, this project also won the Illuminating Engineering Society of North America, International Illumination Design Award – The Paul Waterbury Award for Outdoor Lighting Design Award of Distinction; the International Association of Lighting Designers, Special Citation IALD Award; and the New York Section of the Illuminating Engineering Society of North America, Lumen Award of Merit.

5

7

Opposite

Southeast corner 'blade' armature and studios wall

7 Perforated steel blades display

8 Detail of feature wall elements

Photography: Elliot Kaufman

8

1

NEWMAN HOUSE

2

1   Courtyard
2   Digital façade

St Kilda, Victoria, Australia | Architect: Cassandra Fahey
Engineer: Tim Hall & Associates | 2000

Canterbury Road is a thoroughfare for both trams and cars from St Kilda to the city and vice versa. The strip of land along this road was formerly grassland, petrol stations and tennis courts. The land was subdivided some 10 years ago into lot sizes of around 200 square metres each.

Most of the new dwellings are 'postmodern terraces' – builder-designed derivatives of a derivative of a derivative of something. They become homogenous through their generic use of rendered blue board, colourbond roofs, exposed galvanised 'feature?' balconies, and even more homogenous through the 'Good Design Guide'-inspired decoration, window location, heights and setbacks.

The lot where the Newman House now stands is to the city end of this strip and it is flanked by dwellings that fit the above description. These dwellings had already begun to gain the coat of age that those buildings do before the Newman residence was even conceived of.

The two boundary walls lock the site in, inhibiting north light, but allowing for a vantage to the east – overlooking Albert Park, yet hindered by the light rail between.

It was my early observation that the frontages of the Canterbury Road dwellings were predominantly 'blind'. Closed window screens or small slot windows are all that face the road due to the moderately heavy traffic.

3

4

3 Open-plan living

4 Stair to bedroom

5 Bedroom, glazed bathroom and dressing

6 Aerial view through stairs

7 Detail: mirror under stair

The Newman House beckoned for a blank façade due to the traffic and the client brief. As the client is a well-known Australian television personality he wanted the building to be secure.

A blank façade was part of the schema from early on. In time, and after many versions, it was the Pamela Anderson image that stole the screen.

Due to the now inhibitive bounding walls to the north and south and essentially to the west, it became important to set the building in on the north side of the site, to allow light through the glazed walls, which would separate the interior from an outdoor deck and lap pool.

None of the other houses along this strip have attempted north-facing setbacks due to the immediate lack of saleable square metreage. However it has been essential in imbuing the residence with the light that makes it glow and resonate within.

The use of north-facing glass became instrumental in filling the building with light, while the rear, overlooking the park and light rail, required a different paradoxical strategy: views out, no views in. A reflective glass was used in this instance for two reasons: to present light rail users with a distracting view of themselves and to camouflage the house itself. On the tram, at the speed it travels, one finds it very difficult to either locate the house, or distinguish it from its surroundings.

Upstairs a horizontal Shugg arrangement wraps around the north and east walls, absorbing the morning light and distributing it through the predominantly glazed bathroom. Glass was used internally to allow the transmission of east and north light along the windowless south and west faces.

5

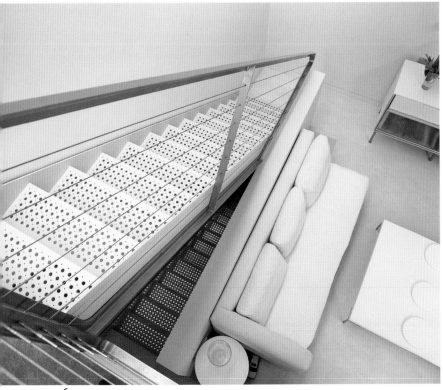

6

7

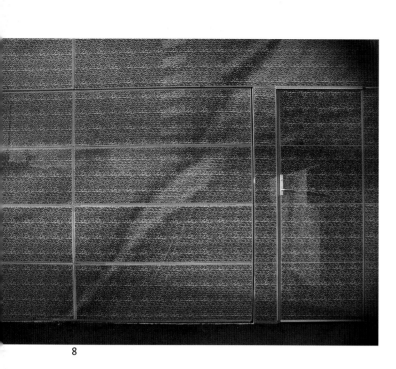

8

8   Garage and pedestrian entry

9   Façade detail

Photography: Peter Hyatt

9

NEWMAN HOUSE

1

NOMENTANA RESIDENCE

2

1 View of entry / library / two-storey impluvium towards hall
2 View of living room towards deck

LOVELL, MAINE, UNITED STATES OF AMERICA | ARCHITECT: MACK SCOGIN MERRILL ELAM ARCHITECTS FORMERLY SCOGIN ELAM AND BRAY ARCHITECTS STRUCTURAL ENGINEER: UZON AND CASE ENGINEERS | 1997

Moving earth, sliding mud, roaring fires, desert brittleness, a long suppressed green deficit are all partial motivations for a coast to coast relocation from Venice Beach, California to Lovell, Maine.

The house realises both a return to the forest and a return to the studio for an artist too long removed from both.

A modest site, 1.1 hectares, yields an intimate view across a pond to Lord's Hill, the eastern-most boundary of the White Mountains National Forest. The hill, an inclined plane approaching the vertical, comforts with summer-spring greenery; dazzles with fall colours; shimmers and glistens in winter snow and ice. Nature ... spectacular in every way that Maine conjures up.

The house perches at the brink of the downward slope to the pond. Breathing in the site, the house transfigures the site through a series of internal spatial events ... framing, focusing, enclosing, extending, dismissing, celebrating ...

Relocated from the farm to the forest, the house refers to and reinterprets the 'big house, little house, back house, barn' of the famous children's rhyme.

Like Maine houses before it, the house is a result of form added on to form, spaces adjoining defensively and closely clustering ... resisting long, harsh Maine winters and giving the impression of small 'house-towns'. Always looking back on itself, the rooms of the house are never alone. They are rooms

NOMENTANA RESIDENCE

3

always in visual and spatial communication. The house is rural and remote but not in isolation.

Programmatic elements include a drawing studio; dog room and runs; living, dining and sitting rooms; library accommodations; kitchen; master suite; guest suite (296 square metres); a two-vehicle garage (42 square metres); a detached painting studio (75.5 square metres); and various porches (98 square metres).

Materials include wood and steel frame on concrete foundations; cementitious fibreboard and pre-weathered zinc cladding; concrete floors; wood and aluminium window and glazing systems.

3 View of hall towards living room / deck / impluvium

4 View of entry / library / two-storey impluvium

5 East–west section facing north

Photography: Timothy Hursley

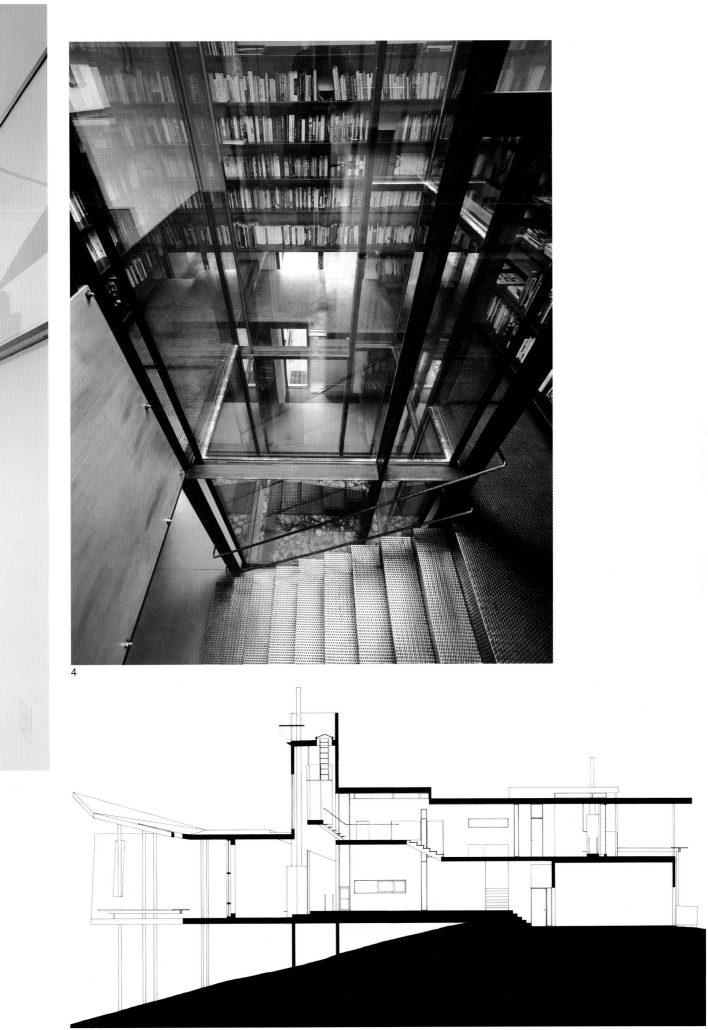

4

5

NOMENTANA RESIDENCE

1

NORTH GERMAN STATE CLEARING BANK BUILDING (NORD LB)

1 Tower rises from internal courtyard
2 Dramatic cantilevers access natural light
3 Connecting footbridge
4 Bright colour accents glass

3

2

4

HANOVER, GERMANY | ARCHITECT: BEHNISCH & PARTNER
STRUCTURAL ENGINEER: PFEFFERKORN & PARTNER | 2002

The building grows out of the exterior perimeter block, reaching a height of 54.8 metres. This high-rise part of the complex detaches itself from the formal order of the city blocks addressing the street, and establishes relationships with a wider context.

The building's central tower is a spiralling superstructure built from masses set at provocative angles. The angles leave various corners cantilevered, a motif continued in other great multileveled masses that appear throughout the visually open composition. The tower overlooks a courtyard tucked away inside the building's six-sided exterior. Below the tower, an enormous triangular slab balcony is set on high posts.

By varying the heights of the complex, a building emerges that gently integrates itself in the existing pattern of the city. The architects designed a building that emerges as a landmark: while the blocks subordinate themselves to the pattern of the environment, the high-rise building develops freely, connecting to more remote features, such as the looser patterns of the city centre.

The architects incorporated the surrounding area's retail, commercial, residential, cultural, sport and leisure establishments into the plan. The desire for a linking element between the city and the residential districts was met by an open and publicly accessible ground-floor concourse

5

5 Main entrance under glass slope

6 Glass tubes connect building segments

7 Conference room

8 Entrance hall

accommodating restaurants, shops and bars in and around the central courtyard. The courtyard is treated as a landscape, with large-scale water elements and plantings establishing further connections to the surroundings.

The reduction of energy consumption and of carbon dioxide emissions by utilising natural resources was one of the major objectives of the building design. Priority was given to window ventilation as the most important source of fresh-air supply to all rooms. Thanks to a double-skin façade on the north side of the block edge and partially on the east and west façades window ventilation is possible even in these noise-exposed areas of the building.

The geothermal chilling potential is exploited by 120 foundation piles with ground heat exchanges consisting of plastic tubes. The tube system inside the concrete ceilings provides for additional cooling. In summer water of roughly 25 degrees Celsius from these ceiling pipes is cooled down in the ground heat exchangers and then made available for cooling purposes.

A daylight redirection system integrated in the external sun-shading system contributes to reducing artificial lighting, allowing the use of direct sunlight without glare problems.

State-of-the-art low-pollutant base-load electricity and heat supply by a fuel cell that also serves as a standby unit is another detail of the building's energy concept. However, the equipment available today is still rather maintenance-intensive.

6

7

8

NORTH GERMAN STATE CLEARING BANK BUILDING (NORD LB)

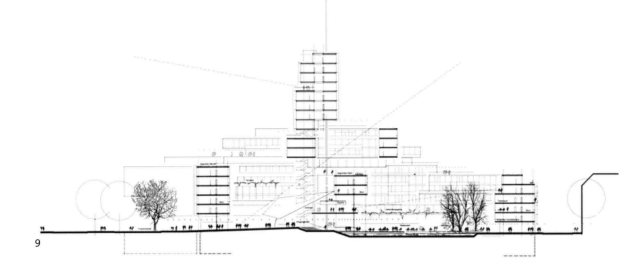

9

10

9 Section
10 Building is between business and residential
11 Water reflects light and glass
12 Geometric play of shapes in glass
13 Executive office

Photography: Roland Halbe

11

12

13

NORTH GERMAN STATE CLEARING BANK BUILDING (NORD LB)

1

OSAKA MARITIME MUSEUM

2

4

3

1 Interior views of the Museum around the Edo-period boat

2&4 Transportation and setting of the Dome from the
construction site to the Osaka Maritime Museum site

3 Exterior view

OSAKA, JAPAN | ARCHITECT: PAUL ANDREU ARCHITECTE
STRUCTURAL ENGINEER: OVE ARUP INTERNATIONAL | 1998

A project found its program and its site at the Osaka Maritime museum. I had already conceived of positioning a semi-circular arch to be mirrored in a huge pond at the French terminal of the cross-channel tunnel and later, I sketched a half-sphere in metal to be reflected in the waters of a port at the foot of a big city. I didn't know which city or which port. I didn't have a precise program. But the idea has stayed with me ever since in a way both vague and defined, as a sort of conceptual homage to Boullée.

Several years later, city planners in charge of the Osaka port decided to construct a building that would waymark the entrance to the port in a new zone of modernised port facilities, leisure activities and more. As in many ports in the world, the new zone crystallises the city's policies of development and reconversion.

Ultimately the decision was made to build an exact replica of an Edo-period boat and to house it in a Maritime Museum with exhibits devoted to the port's history and its future, sea transport in general, boats from different eras, the seas, the winds and so on.

The sphere was a fitting solution. It would encompass the boat while allowing for the creation of circulations all around and underneath, which afford visitors a view of the museum's centrepiece from all angles and at the same time a view of the boats entering and leaving the port.

5

The sphere would look as if it were floating on water and we knew right from the start that if we were to maintain this magical quality, the entrance would have to be from below, by way of a tunnel leading from dry land under water and to the museum. The rest developed gradually thereafter, with the program and the project alternately defining one another until the detailed design stage.

The construction of the glass envelope was of course one of our chief preoccupations. To achieve true transparency, it had to screen out excess light and heat without modifying the colour of the outside light. The frame and ties had to be light yet capable of withstanding exceptionally strong waves. At one point we thought of protecting the sphere with a spherical mobile sunscreen. Using solar energy, it would have moved continuously to face the sun and at the same time it could have been equipped with an automatic glass-cleaning device. It was a magnificent but expensive idea and it was only reasonable to drop it. We designed instead a protection of variable density, integrated into each glass pane as a function of the path described by the sun at critical periods of the year. The sun path analysis was plotted, and then the pattern was scrambled and randomised in the zones of density change so as to obtain

an overall surface pattern with blurred outlines that adds a geometrically complex dimension to the sphere's strict geometrical shape.

The structural glass system

The glass is held together by a 'ten point' system. The use of this system on such a scale is extremely rare, not only in Japan, but in the whole world.

There is no metal frame between the glass sections, just silicone as a sealant to ensure tightness. This makes the whole sphere look like a crystal.

The glass

Most of the glass sections consist of two 15-millimetre glass panes with a sheet of perforated galvanized steel in between. The perforation (10 % —> 100 %) varies in density as a function of the path described by the sun, in order to screen out direct sunrays and reduce air-conditioning to a minimum.

This 'lami metal' also works to create a rich pattern on the outside of the sphere: on sunny days the sphere mirrors the blue sky; in sultry weather, it merges into the choppy grey sea.

6

7

8

5   Detail of structure with glass

6–8   Interior views of the Museum

Photography: Masato Ikuta (1,7), Kawasaki Heavy Industries (2),
Shinkenshiku-sha (3,5,6,8), GA Photographers – Y. Takase (4)

OSAKA MARITIME MUSEUM

1

PARQUE ESPAÑA RESIDENTIAL BUILDING

1 Penthouse
2 Exterior stairs
3 Exterior view from the park

2

3

COLONIA CONDESA, MEXICO CITY | ARCHITECT: TALLER DE ENRIQUE NORTEN ARQUITECTOS, SC (TEN ARQUITECTOS)
STRUCTURAL DESIGN: COLINAS DE BUEN | 2001

The site for this project is in a corner lot in front of a park in a dense urban area in Mexico City.

Six one-family, one-storey lofts (except the uppermost residence which is a double-storey penthouse), sit on top of a contemporary art gallery. A 14-car garage occupies the ground floor.

Open, free plans allow for future residents to design and accommodate the space to their own desires and necessities. All services – fixed – are accommodated in a continuous block in the eastern interior section of the building. The floor plate extends to the south – park views – by a cantilevered terrace.

The street façade – most likely to be occupied by the bedrooms – is sheltered by a slim balcony of aluminium grid with sliding partitions of translucent fabric that provide light diffusion and sun protection to the west-oriented elevation, privacy where needed and an ever-changing random order that varies constantly.

All residents will share a roof garden with wooden deck flooring and a lap pool. The service stairs connect every level, and a spiral staircase that connects with the roof garden composes the back façade. Access to the lofts from the stairs occurs through a bridge.

4

5

6

7

4 Interior
5 Façade's stairs
6&7 Exterior view
Photography: Jaime Navarro

1

PICTURE WINDOW HOUSE

2

1 Glass panels open on either side of the main living space creating a continuity from the woods behind the house to the sea below

2 The structure allows for a 20-metre clear span on the lower level. Above, are bathrooms doubling as a corridor.

IZU, SHIZUOKA, JAPAN | ARCHITECT: SHIGERU BAN ARCHITECTS
STRUCTURAL ENGINEER: HOSHINO ARCHITECT & ENGINEER | 2002

A gentle hill continues up from the ocean's edge, and near its peak is the location of the site; a place that, amazingly in Japan, is uncluttered by any unsightly distractions. The first time I set foot on the site, my immediate response was to frame the wonderful view of the ocean stretching horizontally. That is to say that the building itself should become a picture window. Also, to prevent the architecture from becoming an obstacle disrupting the natural sense of flow from the ocean, I've thought of maintaining that continuity by passing it through the building up to the woods at the top of the hill. Thus, the whole upper storey became a truss spanning 20 metres, and below, a 20-metre by 2.5-metre picture window was created.

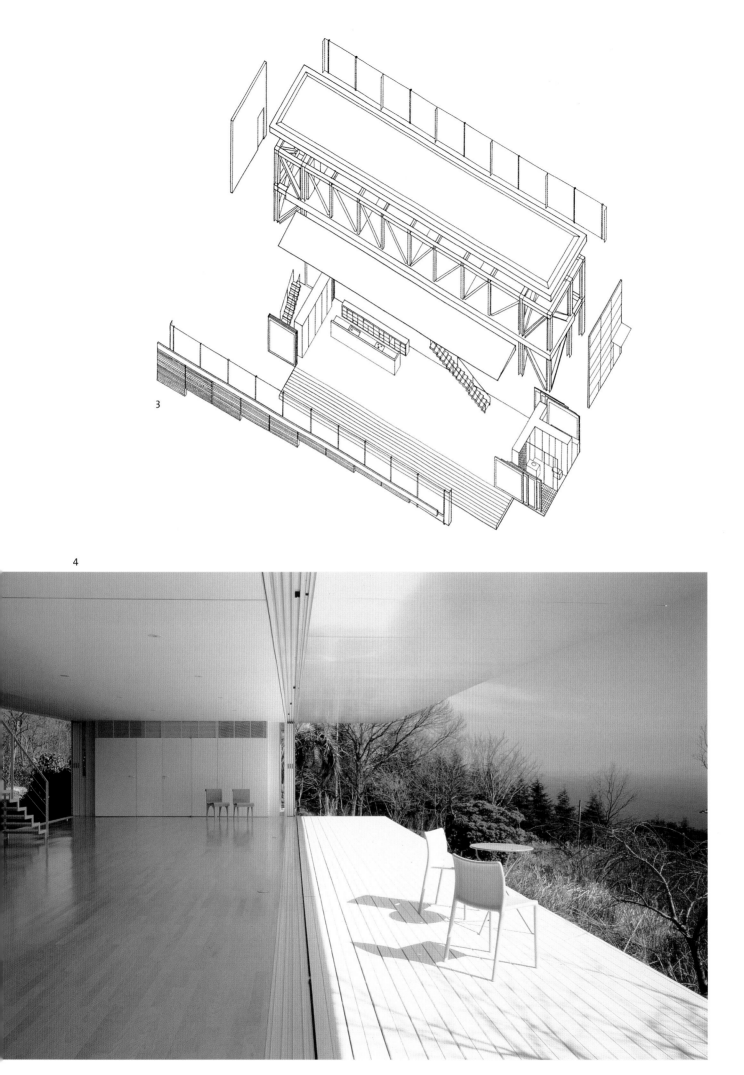

3

4

5

6

3   Conceptual axonometric drawing

4   View of main living space extending outside as a rail-less terrace

5   View of bathroom looking down the corridor

6   Interior view of a bedroom upstairs. Diagonal braces of the structure are exposed inside the room.

Following pages

   Exterior view with visible truss structure in upper level and on either end. Exterior aluminium blinds
   line the bedrooms in the upper level.

Photography: Hiroyuki Hirai

1

PORTLAND INTERNATIONAL AIRPORT

1 Pedestrian bridges link the parking garage and terminal

2 A steel and glass canopy shelters the drop-off area and passage from the parking structure to the terminal

3 East–west section through canopy

2

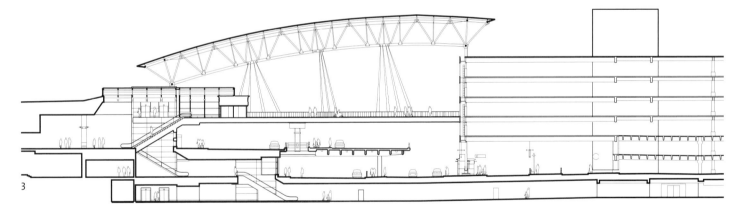

3

PORTLAND, OREGON, UNITED STATES OF AMERICA | ARCHITECT: ZIMMER GUNSUL FRASCA PARTNERSHIP STRUCTURAL ENGINEER: KPFF CONSULTING ENGINEERS | 2002

Like cities, it is rare that an airline terminal is built at one point in time from whole cloth. Most airline terminals, like cities, expand and change over long periods of time as needs increase and times change.

Such is the terminal for a mid-size city in the Pacific Northwest. The original terminal, built in 1957, realised its first expansion in the mid-1970s and presently is surrounded and buried within the new construction. Nevertheless, it determined the location of principal terminal elements (runways, gate locations, floor-to-floor height and so on). The work shown here that began in the last decade, and was recently completed, is the work of a single architectural team and was accomplished in three, more or less, uninterrupted phases.

The phases include three new concourses and two concourse lobbies, a terminal expansion of the upper level ticketing area and the lower level baggage handling; a new parking structure and roadway expansion which includes two pedestrian bridges to the parking structure and a roadway canopy. Included in the last phase was an extension of the light rail system that connects to much of the metropolitan area and a station adjacent to the terminal. A future concourse expansion to the south will fully incorporate the station.

The extensive use of glass in the terminal provides natural light and creates connections to the outdoors, which help orient passengers. Glass is first utilised outside the airport, where a

4

5

11,148-square-metre steel and glass canopy arches over the roadway between the garage and the terminal. Inside the facility, skylights and large windows exaggerate the amount of light in the interior spaces. An angled glass wall on the terminal façade brightens the ticketing and baggage claim areas, while large skylights flood the north and south lobbies with light. Both lobbies feature a wall of glass that opens the view to airport runways and the lush Oregon landscape. Smaller skylights punctuate the airport's concourses.

Clarity and convenience for the passenger, while accommodating airline needs, was the principal design generator. A singular image accomplished over a long period of time is a testament to the clarity of leadership that three separate client administrations provided over this period of time.

4   Art installations by Larry Kirkland in Concourse C

5   North terminal lobby

6   South terminal lobby

7   North–south section though Concourse C

8   Departures level

Photography: Eckert & Eckert (4,6,8), Timothy Hursley (1,2), Strode Eckert Photographic (5)

6

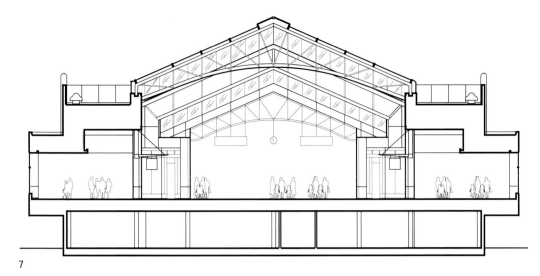

7

8

1

2

SINGAPORE ARTS CENTRE

3

1   Night view of Concert Hall across harbour

2   Concert Hall foyer and building enclosure

3   Three-dimensional glazed enclosure to Opera House and
    Concert Hall foyers

SINGAPORE | ARCHITECT: MICHAEL WILFORD & PARTNERS, LONDON
IN ASSOCIATION WITH DP ARCHITECTS PTE LTD, SINGAPORE
STRUCTURAL ENGINEER: SINGAPORE PUBLIC WORKS DEPARTMENT | 2002

We believe that architecture should transcend the functional characteristics of activity container and climate modifier and should be a cultural symbol and physical manifestation of society's values, aspirations and way of life. To establish an appropriate architectural design for the Arts Centre project, we have considered both cultural and physical contexts.

Much of recent architecture fails to respond to the rich cultural diversity arising out of its geographic location and history. The pursuit of better economic and social conditions through modernisation has marginalised traditions. So, in addition to expressing technology and responding to climate, architecture

needs to re-establish cultural continuity with the past in order to hypothesise about the future. History tells us who we are, what we have achieved and provides a rich resource of types and precedents.

Recent developments in drama, dance and music in Singapore have demonstrated that an appropriate fusion between modern techniques and local traditions can localise external influences and invigorate the ethnic cultures. Both can co-exist and reinforce each other. The design of the Arts Centre is intended to express this fusion.

The Centre will occupy a magnificent 4-hectare site in Marina Park between Marina Centre and Marina Bay with four contrasting edge conditions: formal frontage to the Padang and Civic District; dramatic downtown views across Marina Bay; informal face to Marina Square across Raffles Avenue; and open views along Marina Park to the sea. It is well connected to all parts of the island by a network of arterial roads and close to Raffles City MRT Station.

Future extension of the central business district into Marina South will produce a horseshoe of downtown towers enclosing three sides of the Bay and focused towards the Arts Centre. A symbolic dialogue and balance can thus be established between commerce and culture.

Our aim has been to create a unique and dynamic Arts Centre that satisfies the functional requirements of the brief, responds to the fabric and scale of surrounding buildings and stimulates the imagination and participation of the community. The challenge is to produce a design that represents the future as well as the past through an evolution of traditions rather than use of historical pastiche. The design is a unique assembly of forms and spaces expressing the range of the building's significance from abstract cultural symbol, focal piece of the city fabric, to a myriad of personal experiences.

As landmark and urban focus, the Singapore Arts Centre will have a distinct identity. It will help define and strengthen the adjacent Civic/Cultural District and enhance its function as the venue for national celebrations and ceremonies. Various stages of land reclamation have progressively detached the Bras Basah corridor and Padang from their original seashore location. The centre of the city has thus lost its direct relationship with the point at which it was first established. The Arts Centre will reconnect the city to the sea (as now represented by Marina Bay).

4

4   Upper part of main entrance foyer

5   Interior of Concert Hall looking towards orchestra platform

6   Detail of sun-screening and building enclosure with city high-rises beyond

7   View out of Concert Hall foyer into city centre

8   Shadow pattern on Opera House wall from sun-screening

Photography: Euijin Goh; Jonathon Rose

5

6

8

7

1

2

1 View from south

2 Entry

3 Southwest-facing court

Photography: Tim Hursley

SOFTWARE MANUFACTURER

3

FARGO, NORTH DAKOTA, UNITED STATES OF AMERICA | ARCHITECT: JULIE
SNOW ARCHITECT INC.
STRUCTURAL ENGINEER: ARUP | 2002

Removed from traditional high-tech regions, this software manufacturer chose to locate on the flat Dakota prairie of the north central United States. High-bandwidth global access is leveraged to allow a sustained physical connection to this boundless plains landscape, which the company sees as emblematic of the individual's unrestricted creative opportunity.

The buildings are detailed to reinforce an experiential connection with navigating the expansive space of the plains. A slight gap visually separates the beam and column, with the connection occurring as a vertical plate concealed in the raised floor. Floor and ceiling planes pull back from the curtainwall, with the mullion aligned with the structural deck, below the

floor level. The resulting sensation is of floating within a glass box which itself floats within the landscape. The simultaneous navigation and connection to this extremely flat landscape underscores the company's paradoxical rural/global identity.

Despite the large expanses of glass, the building is designed to perform efficiently in this harsh climate. Distributed mechanical equipment towers deliver low pressure 65-degree air through a raised floor system controlled individually by hand-operated floor louvres. Outside air is used later in the spring and earlier in the fall, reducing cooling loads. Higher spaces allow diffused daylighting, improving its distribution and reducing glare. An airier, more comfortable space is the result.

1

SOLAR TUBE

1 South elevation
2 North (entrance) elevation

DÖBLING, VIENNA, AUSTRIA | ARCHITECT: GEORG DRIENDL ARCHITEKT
STRUCTURAL ENGINEER: D.I. ERNST ILLETSCHKO | 2001

The property, where Solar Tube was built, is situated in Döbling, a northwestern outskirt of Vienna. Döbling is a quiet, rather wealthy residential area with mostly single-family homes. The property itself is rather narrow but long with a high tree stock. The size of the property totals 1,300 square metres.

Before the actual design process could be started, the opportunities had to be checked. The opportunities are always defined by the characteristics of the location, the plot and the landscape. The sun's position was taken into account as well as the number of hours of sunlight and a range of other weather aspects before starting the actual design process.

Why 'solar tube'?

A 'solar tube' in general is a small light-and-heat captor which is usually installed on the roofs of houses. In this case, the entire house serves as a collector, opening to light and heat on all sides. The wooded site has enabled the architect to use generously glazed elevations, which are sloping or curved in various parts. Since the roof and floors are also partly transparent, the core of the house works like an integrated atrium. As for the glass 'tube' that forms the uppermost level, it helps cut heating costs in winter. Apart from its energy-saving virtues, glass also offers intimacy with the surrounding nature. Therefore one gets the feeling of living in a treehouse. It's a symbiosis between nature and architecture.

3

4

5

Built in only five months

Solar Tube was built in only five months, from April until August 2001. This fast construction was possible due to the usage of mostly prefabricated or in-stock units and base materials. Custom-designed and manufactured elements do not necessarily produce better results. At the same time, choosing an alternative solution saves a lot of money, energy and time. We have always been supporters of fast and efficient construction.

Low energy concept

Overheating in summer is avoided by the trees as well as by a special ventilation system that works like a chimney. In winter the heating costs can be cut to a minimum because of the compact coat of the building that is designed in a way of absorption and reflection that allow a high amount of sun energy to be used. On the other hand, of course, the defoliated trees in winter allow the sunlight to shine through the glazed façade and roof and therefore also help cut the heating costs.

Design and functionality

Seeing 'solar tube' from the street is an experience on its own. Passers-by are attracted by the remarkable shape of the house as well as by the glass façade, although the façade facing the street is more closed (compared to the sides facing the garden) to give the inhabitants more intimacy.

The integrated atrium that builds the core of the house is open to all sides. Even from the ground level one can see through to the sliding roof. This is possible due to the partly transparent floors on one hand and on the other hand due to the fact that the bedrooms in the uppermost level are reached over a gallery. The interior is also characterised by the spirit of 'open living'. All of the integrated furniture (kitchen, library, integrated cupboards, bathrooms and so on) was also designed by our office and therefore fits in perfect harmony to the design of the building itself.

6

7

8

9

9   South elevation/terrace
10   Kitchen/living room
11   Library/gallery

Photography: James Morris/Axiom Photo Agency; Bruno Klomfar

10

11

1

SONDICA AIRPORT NEW TERMINAL

2

3

4

1 View of the parking

2&3 View of the hall

4 General view of the airport from west

Photography: Paolo Rosselli

BILBAO, SPAIN │ ARCHITECT: SANTIAGO CALATRAVA S.A.
STRUCTURAL ENGINEER: SANTIAGO CALATRAVA │ 2000

By 1990, Sondica Airport had reached the limits of its development. Located to the north of Bilbao, on the coast of the Bay of Biscay, the facility had been built to cope only with domestic flights and could not function as a transportation hub for the growing Basque region north of Bilbao. The Spanish airport authorities accordingly asked Calatrava to design a new terminal with four embarkation gates, which would comply with international air-transport standards. In 1994, in response to the increased number of flights to this quickly developing area, the authorities requested a second, enlarged proposal for passenger facilities, this time with a total of eight gates.

Located approximately 10 kilometres north of the city, with a metro connection planned, the new airport is situated across the airfield from the original terminal. Within this new facility, there is considerable potential for future expansion. Sondica Airport is able to handle two million passengers per year as of the year 2000, and it will ultimately be able to accommodate up to 10 million.

The organisational and architectural centre of the complex is a large glazed hall. As the steel structure of the aerodynamic roof sweeps upwards in the direction of the airfield, it spans the administrative areas, restaurants and waiting areas. Located behind the canted glazed façades, these waiting areas directly overlook the apron and runways. The triangular plan of the hall follows the natural flow of passengers towards a transverse linear walkway that leads to the gates.

A generously curved, glazed entrance on the north side of the terminal allows full use of the 36-metre traffic drop-off area. The elevated, upper level of this vehicle access is for departures; the lower level is for arrivals. In non-glazed areas, the concrete structure of the east and west wings is clad in a unifying skin of aluminium.

The airport is connected by a 100-metre subterranean passageway to a four-storey parking garage, which can accommodate 1,500 vehicles. The garage is partially recessed into a landscaped rise. In this way, the parking structure is integrated into the complex both functionally and visually, as is too rarely the case at airports. In another design initiative that will encourage overall coherence, Calatrava's plan for the airport accommodates provisions for the future construction of auxiliary facilities, such as hotels and a recreational complex.

2

1 View towards *kijinguchi* and *toko* from tatami room

2 Downward view from north

3 View through tatami room towards *katteguchi* on south

4 West elevation

5 View from garden on west

6 View towards *toko* from tatami room

1

3

TEA HOUSE (FUKYO)

4

5

6

YAMAGUCHI, JAPAN │ ARCHITECT: HIROYUKI ARIMA + URBAN FOURTH
STRUCTURAL ENGINEER: FUKUOKA KOUZOU │ 2001

The Fukyo Tea House comprises a three-mat tatami room and a large staging area, which is a suitable space not only for tea ceremonies, but other activities usually performed by a hotel, such as parties, weddings, shows, concerts, meetings and dinners.

Tatami mats are the only traditional material to be found in the tea house; it is mainly composed of common, easily obtainable industrial materials that relate more readily to modern buildings. The use of these materials is also related to the architects' desire for communication and transparency. Materials used for interior and exterior spaces include transparent glass, translucent glass, stainless steel sheeting, stainless steel mesh, monochrome paint and timber.

Seven moveable panels define the interior spaces of the tea house. The panels can revolve, swing or slide, depending on the desired use of the space.

Text, written by Tomomi Fujiwara, is scattered on the walls and on the moveable panels. Whether or not the text can be seen by guests depends on the orientation of the moveable panels.

The undulating yard is planted with maple trees. A pathway leads into the maples, and doubles as the approach to the house.

7

8

9

10

7 View towards tatami room with rotating door
   in foreground

8 View towards *nijiriguchi* from tatami room

9 *Katteguchi* on west

10 View from southwest

Photography: Kouji Okamoto

1

TROYES MEDIATHEQUE (MÉDIATHÈQUE DE L'AGGLOMÉRATION TROYENNE)

2

3

1 The blue 'screen-façade' facing east
2 Entrance to the médiathèque under the canopy
3 South and east façades

TROYES, FRANCE | ARCHITECT: DU BESSET-LYON ARCHITECTES
STRUCTURAL ENGINEER: KHEPHREN INGÉNIERIE | 2002

The unflattering siting of the Troyes public library, to the rear of a McDonald's restaurant, is in stark contrast to the importance of the collection of national treasures housed inside. The location led the architects to concentrate on the interior of the building, so as not to compete or even interact with the surrounding buildings. The geometry of the building is deliberately uncertain and elusive; the exterior makes no statement, and the distinctions between interior and exterior are deliberately blurred.

The library incorporates a main public area, information counter, children's library with story-telling space; book storage on three levels with a fire-proof glass façade, a cafeteria, a glass-walled historical collection surrounded by ramps and a viewing platform, reading rooms and administrative offices.

The interior forms its own urban landscape with the incorporation of large-scale elements, and effectively negates any sense of the external environment. One of these dominant elements is a glittering, gold-coloured, undulating steel mesh suspended false ceiling, which covers the entire first floor. A pink staircase is immediately apparent once inside the plain façade. Yet another element is an artwork text by Lawrence Weiner that appears on the yellow glazing separating the children's reading zone from the ground floor corridor. The blue text is over 50 metres long and relates to the connection between writing and objects ('written in the heart of objects').

4

These oversize elements create a sense of openness. Far from overwhelming, they are transparent and colourful in nature and add to the overall impression of substance and depth; their size encourages visitors to explore and walk around them in order to appreciate them fully. The architects' desire is that this exploration and the acquired impressions will serve as a metaphor for reading.

5

4   Main façade showing the depth of the médiathèque

5   Blue screen and golden ceiling

6&7   Reading-room on the first floor

8   Reading-room on the first floor under the golden canopy

6

7

8

TROYES MEDIATHEQUE (MÉDIATHÈQUE DE L'AGGLOMÉRATION TROYENNE)

10

11

9 The old wooden reading-room on the first floor

10 The hall with pink stairway and sentence

11 The exterior extention of the golden ceiling

Photography: Philippe Ruault

TROYES MEDIATHEQUE (MÉDIATHÈQUE DE L'AGGLOMÉRATION TROYENNE)

1

UPTOWN MÜNCHEN

2

3

1 Fantastic views across city and countryside

2 The high-rise has become a new landmark for Munich

3 The 146-metre high-rise is accompanied by five campus
   buildings, each 29 metres high

MUNICH, GERMANY │ ARCHITECT: INGENHOVEN OVERDIEK ARCHITEKTEN, DÜSSELDORF
STRUCTURAL ENGINEER: BURGGRAF, WEICHINGER & PARTNER, MUNICH │ 2004

No sooner had the high-rise debate in Germany, grown silent during the office space surplus in the nineties, regained momentum – especially in Munich, known for its hostility towards high-rise development – when the destruction of the World Trade Towers in New York on 11 September 2001 brought it to a sudden halt.

The Uptown München project had already been launched after a lengthy process of debates and permit applications. In the Bavarian metropolis, rather conservative in matters of architecture, the project that signalled in a new phase of high-rise construction on the Isar River, this project is one of superlatives. Construction on the office complex on the Mittlerer Ring city highway began at the end of September

2001. The sheer size of the complex – 84,000 square metres gross floor area – worried no one, although it had sparked heated debates on one particular aspect. How high, people asked, should one allow the tower of the complex to rise to reach into Bavaria's famous blue and white sky? There is a general consensus that the towers of the Frauenkirche should determine the scale in Munich, that no other building should surpass them in height. Yet even the most determined opponents were unable to halt high-rise development on the Mittlerer Ring beyond the boundary of the core. BMW still stayed below the 100-metre-mark of the sacrosanct onion towers, but the fall from grace came in 1975 with the construction of the 114-metre-tall Hypobank. The client was finally granted permission to top his Uptown München project at 146 metres – most likely a precedent-setting decision for other ambitious plans in the future. This project evolved from another design by the architects for the same site. The basic urban planning concept and thus the further principles for the design had already been determined by the municipal authority. However, the new client's use requirements for the high-rise meant that a new design was necessary.

The Mittlerer Ring, the city's busiest traffic artery, is already dotted with other prominent landmarks: the Hypobank tower, the BMW building and the TV tower. But Uptown Munich will soon take pride of place as the tallest office building. The client is far more interested in the prestige of the site in immediate proximity to the Olympic park with good links to highways, airport and subway.

The 38-storey tower is flanked by a campus of seven-storey office tracts. A boulevard connects the buildings and glass walls between the gables protect against noise emissions. Restaurants, cafés and shops line the path from the subway station to the offices and give the entire district a certain level of autonomy.

The landmark tower will introduce a novel look. The glass skin envelops the load-bearing structure like a stretched membrane. Contrary to what has become the standard in the past years, the façade is conceived as a single-leaf building skin without the usual, climate-efficient cavity to accommodate wind-protected shading elements. New sunscreen glass, with excellent insulation values, protects against unwanted insolation and overheating. Internal anti-glare components, combined with corresponding ventilation measures, contribute to efficient construction. Apart from the reduced construction costs, this approach translates into significant savings in operating expenses, by halving the area of glass that requires cleaning.

The glass skin is designed to allow for visual contact both from the inside out and vice versa, investing the tower with an unusual lightness and transparency. Natural ventilation is provided for each occupant's individual control through motor-driven circular, parallel tilt windows.

The office areas in the tower are flexible for a wide variety of layouts and uses. Single-, group- and open-plan offices with a respectable clearance of 3 metres are feasible, as is the division into smaller rental units.

The tower will offer stunning panoramic views. The ever-changing spectacle of the weather, the vista across city and countryside, and beyond all the way to the 50-kilometre-long panorama of the Alps may even distract some occupants from their work. The upper levels, in particular, will benefit as executive floors furnished with lobbies and observation areas.

4

4 A boulevard connects the buildings and glass walls between the gables protect against noise emissions

5 The glazed corners, rounded in plan and at the head of the building, are characteristic features of the high-rise

6 Ground floor

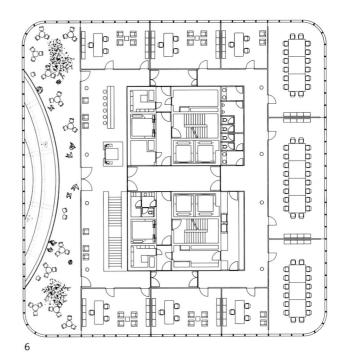

6

5

7

8

9

10

7   View along Georg-Brauchle-Ring

8   Section

9   The single-leaf façade will be equipped with electronically
    operated round tilt windows for natural ventilation in the
    office areas

10 Every other façade component contains one such window

Photography: H. G. Esch, Hennef / Ingenhoven Overdiek Architekten,
Düsseldorf

1

THE WESTIN NEW YORK AT TIMES SQUARE

1   8th Avenue elevation showing window spandrels beginning at 42nd floor forming a map of Times Square

2   A checkerboard of glass windows punctures a large-scale abstract origami-style design on the mid-rise suite section of the hotel that juts out in front of the towers along 42nd Street on the south side

3   'Brush strokes' of coloured glass add depth and dimension to the buildings skin giving a painterly effect

2

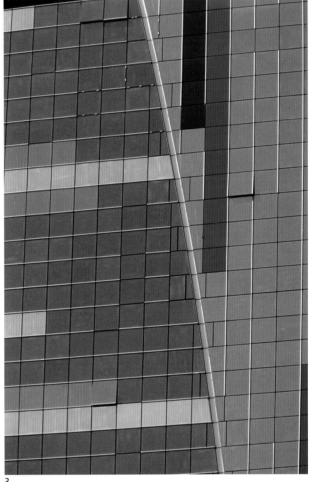

3

NEW YORK, NEW YORK, UNITED STATES OF AMERICA | ARCHITECT: ARQUITECTONICA
ARCHITECT OF RECORD: HKS INCORPORATED | STRUCTURAL ENGINEER: YSRAEL A. SEINUK; MEP
JAROS BAUM AND BOLLES | 2001

Using more than 1,000 permutations of curtain wall panels and intricate patterns of coloured glass inspired by 'earth' and 'sky' tones, the façade of The Westin New York at Times Square cuts a distinctive presence with a soaring beam of light arching up its northern and southern faces.

The design, fabrication and installation process required strict co-ordination and execution by each participant. The project has linked specialists and high-quality materials from around the world, with affiliates of New York-based Tishman Realty & Construction, Co., Inc. as developer/owner/builder, Miami-based Arquitectonica as design architect, the Italian façade expert Permasteelisa Cladding Technologies as curtain wall

fabricator and installer and Viracon, a leading producer of high-quality professional glass.

The wide-ranging efforts to create this architectural 'work of art' began with the creative and far-reaching design drawn by Arquitectonica, followed by a painstaking effort by Tishman and its design team to create working models for each portion of the façade. The effort then shifted to Permasteelisa, which had its aluminium extrusions made in Italy and painted in Holland, and to Viracon, which produced the 8,000 glass lites to high standards of quality at its high-tech Minnesota factory.

The Westin New York's 17,094 square metres of curtain wall consists of approximately 4,500 panels, with almost 1,000

4

4 The forms are bifurcate at the top creating a distinctive skyline; the recess between them contains a beam of light that shoots upwards into the city skies

5 42nd Street south elevation where two distinct sculptural forms emerge: one broadening towards the sky, the other anchoring to the ground. The vertical tower is clad in vertically striated steel blue glass and the anchored tower in horizontally striated bronze glass.

Photography: Norman McGrath

panel permutations among the various shapes, connection devices, colours and sizes of both frames and glass. This extensive variety has required the fabrication and installation team to imprint each part of each panel with barcodes to ensure proper matching of pieces and placement of the panels onto the façade.

Arquitectonica chose the pattern, colours, shapes and location of the panels. The design expresses the meeting of earth and sky, with copper, gold and rust highlights to represent the earth, and silver, blue, purple and aqua to represent the sky. In selecting the glass, Arquitectonica chose lites with reflectivity values that allow the façade to approximate a monolithic abstract painting on the entire curtain wall.

The panels have several main parts: the extruded aluminium alloy frame, the vision or spandrel glass lites, sealants and adhesives, insulation, galvanised steel and the connector bracket assembly.

5

THE WESTIN NEW YORK AT TIMES SQUARE

INDEX